Loyd Grossman's
Italian Journey

Loyd Grossman's Italian Journey

Discover the taste
of regional Italy, with over
60 easy-to-follow recipes

VERMILION
LONDON

1 3 5 7 9 10 8 6 4 2

Text copyright © Loyd Grossman 1994
Photographs copyright © Loyd Grossman 1994

First published in the United Kingdom in 1994 by Vermilion
an imprint of Ebury Press
Random House
20 Vauxhall Bridge Road, London SW1V 2SA

Random House Australia (Pty) Limited
20 Alfred Street, Milsons Point, Sydney,
New South Wales 2061, Australia

Random House New Zealand Limited
18 Poland Road, Glenfield,
Auckland 10, New Zealand

Random House South Africa (Pty) Limited
PO Box 337, Bergvlei, South Africa

Random House UK Limited Reg. No. 954009

A CIP catalogue record for this book is available
from the British Library.

ISBN: 0 09 178549 9

Designed and produced by Tucker Slingsby
London House, 66 Upper Richmond Road, London SW15 2RP

Printed and bound in Italy by New Interlitho S.p.a., Milan

Papers used by Ebury Press are natural recyclable products made
from wood grown in sustainable forests.

Foreword

I asked the very nice folks at Granada Television if I could spend a month travelling around Italy eating and they said: 'yes'. Oh, but there was one tiny hitch: I had to make a television series about it. Fortunately, Nicky Taylor, who had directed my previous **This Morning** strand about French cooking agreed to work with me again. Not too long after that, Nicky, Ailsa Greenhaigh (our researcher), Mike Blakeley (our cameraman), Ian Hills (our sound recordist) and I were sitting by the seaside in Positano eating spaghetti alle vongole.

A ten-part series filmed in what I feel is one of the very greatest food countries in the world was, of necessity, going to be very subjective and perhaps as notable for what was left out as what was put in. We chose ten areas that would take us across the boot in a north-easterly direction, beginning south of Naples and ending up in Venice. We could have just as easily started in Liguria and crossed Italy in a south-easterly direction ending up in Puglia. As someone who has visited Italy regularly for 20 years, I was acutely aware that we would only scratch the surface of an amazingly rich and complex way of living and eating. I hope that we will be lucky enough to be sent back to Italy to make some further programmes.

All of the recipes in this book say something about a particular regional or local way of cooking. They come from real Italian cooks and I hope that readers will find them full of equally real flavours. The lesson for any of us who enjoys cooking is to perform in the kitchen with confidence, simplicity and, perhaps the most distinctive hallmark of Italian cookery, generosity. As a cook, you should make yourself, your family and friends happy.

We could not have made the programmes and I could

not have written this book without the enthusiasm, knowledge and hospitality of many people throughout Italy, and this book is gratefully dedicated to them.

The programmes and the book owe much of their form and wit to Nicky Taylor, and it would all have been very different indeed without the hard work and talent of Ailsa, Mike and Ian. There are times in the book when I use the pronoun 'we': I assure you that I am not being regal about myself, I'm just referring to the team.

Finally, if you haven't been to Italy yet, I urge you to go there. Until then, I hope that this book gives you some idea of what this enchanting country is like.

Acknowledgements

Many thanks to the following who provided recipes, valuable local knowledge and generally looked after us with immense generosity:

Le Sirenuse, Positano
Hotel Giordano e Villa
  Maria, Ravello
Hotel Excelsior, Naples
Dal Francese, Norcia
Hotel La Posta, Norcia
Le Pentegramma, Spoleto
Castello di Spaltenna,
  Gaiole in Chianti
Castello di Monsanto,
  Monsanto
Villa La Massa, Candeli
Cantinetta Antinori,
  Florence
Vecchia Lugana, Lugana
Villa del Quar, Verona

Maso Doss, Sant' Antonio
  di Mavignola
Castel Toblino
Beccherie, Treviso
Tony del Spin, Treviso
Villa Corner della Regina,
  Cavasagra
Hotel Cipriani, Venice
Harry's Bar, Venice
Villa Gaidello Club,
  Castelfranco Emilia
Grand Hotel Baglioni,
  Bologna
Ristorante Biagi, Bologna
Fiorucci Foods

and thanks to Italian Escapades, Citroen U.K., the Italian State Tourist Office (London) and its regional offices throughout Italy.

Contents

From Positano to San Marzano

We are sitting on the very beautiful terrace of the Sirenuse Hotel in Positano about 60 kilometres down the coast from Naples. Antonio and Franco Sersale, the father and son team who own the hotel, are giving me some basic instructions in pasta cooking and eating.

'What you must never do is drink anything other than water with pasta,' Antonio sternly tells me, pouring out more glasses of white wine to drink with our spaghetti alle vongole. 'It is a rule that every Italian knows and no Italian follows,' he laughs.

Pasta, like every other food in Italy – from the cheapest and most basic right up through to the most arcane and expensive – is circumscribed by an incredibly elaborate set of rules and folklore governing its purchase, preparation and consumption. Whoever you talk to in Italy about food – and everyone in Italy talks about food all the time – will be laying down some sort of gastronomic law which will invariably be disregarded just like Antonio's no-wine-with-pasta law. In Italy the propensity to make rules and the propensity to break rules are equally strong. Just look at their tax system!

Food reflects culture. Cooking isn't merely about making something nice to eat; it's the product of geography, history and religion. Italy is paradoxically an old place and a young country: it didn't exist as a nation until 1861. Before that, the boot was one of the world's great battle-grounds as city states, kingdoms, empires and the papacy, all vied for control of this rich and rugged peninsula that commands the Mediterranean.

Italy may have been unified politically, but gastronomic unification never followed. What we somewhat crudely call 'Italian cooking' is really a patchwork of local and regional

Antonio Sersale enjoying spaghetti alle vongole at the Sirenuse Hotel

cuisines, all fiercely claiming to be the best in the country. As a hungry traveller in Italy you tend to say that the dish you are eating at the time is undoubtedly the best to be found anywhere, from the Alps to Sicily: it's always polite and usually true.

Positano lies at the beginning of one of the most spectacular stretches of coastline in a country of spectacular coastlines. The Apennine mountains, the rocky spine that runs down the back of Italy, run straight into the sea at the Gulf of Salerno. The precipitous hillsides and small harbours are home to the world famous resorts of Positano, Amalfi and Ravello. Longfellow, Ibsen, Wagner and John Steinbeck have been some of the more well-known devotees of the Amalfi coast, whose colourful, high-priced villages and startlingly blue waters continue to attract the artistic as well as the merely rich and famous.

Although the towns of the Amalfi coast have all had their moments of political glory, the dominant local power was the Kingdom of the Two Sicilies based in Naples. As a result, the local cooking is heavily influenced by Neapolitan ideas. This whole area, all part of the Campania region, is devoted to the flavours of olive oil, red chillies and seafood.

A dizzy climb below the Sirenuse Hotel is one of Positano's fishmongers, displaying three different types of clam as well as sea bream, little red mullet and totani, or flying squid. Seafood figures heavily on local menus – fried, grilled, or with pasta. The emblematic dish of the Campania coast has to be pasta (usually spaghetti) alle vongole, with clams. It comes in two varieties, red and white. Partisans of white clam sauce sniff that tomatoes ruin the taste: 'the tomato is far too greedy to put with the delicate flavour of clams,' a local cook would declare. I'm so greedy I like it either way. But it all has to begin with properly cooked pasta.

There is more guff and nonsense written about pasta than almost any other food. Cooking it is not a mysterious ritual. First let me say something about the difference between fresh and dried pasta. Unfortunately because 'fresh' has more positive connotations than 'dried', a lot of English speaking people think that fresh pasta is superior to dried pasta. Absolutely not. Different yes, but superior no. In the south, pasta is almost invariably dried and mass produced from nothing more than high quality durum wheat and water. Buy it from a top class Italian manufacturer – and pasta is so cheap that it is pointless to cut corners – and you will have the same pasta that is served up by some of the best cooks in Italy.

To cook it, you will need a very large saucepan full of boiling water that has been heavily salted with coarse or rock salt. Put the pasta into the water, and as it softens and slips below the surface, stir it well to separate the strands. Do not add oil to the water in the mistaken belief that it will keep the pasta from sticking together, just stir the pasta frequently as it cooks.

When is it done? When it tastes right. All over Italy pasta is served 'al dente' which means nothing more than 'firm to the bite'. As you get used to eating proper pasta you will discover that firm pasta tastes much better than stuff that has been boiled to hell and back. Most packets of pasta will have a cooking time indicated on them and until you're confident, it's worth following the manufacturer's instructions. As soon as the pasta is cooked, it has to be taken out of its cooking water. There are of course two 'correct' ways to do this. Either lift the pasta out of the water and into a warmed serving dish, or drain it in a colander. Take my word for it, the colander is easier.

Don't leave pasta hanging around: get it sauced and served as quickly as possible. As with draining, there are two 'correct' ways of saucing pasta. One way is to put the sauce onto the pasta as the pasta sits in its serving dish. The other way is to put the pasta into the pan containing the hot sauce and to shake, stir and toss the pan vigorously until the two are combined. I think the second way makes more sense as it keeps the pasta hotter, but it's up to you.

Positano is jet set in the nicest possible way, with a superabundance of luxurious hotels, smart boutiques and top hole sports cars coexisting alongside the obvious charms

Pasta being prepared at San Marzano

of an ancient hillside port. A short but terrifying drive down the vertiginous coast road, Ravello is just as much a magnet for tourists but noticeably less glitzy. Many people boast – sometimes truthfully – about having had a great-great-great-grandfather who was a millionaire but lost all his money through drink, gambling or a bad marriage. And many now relatively sleepy Italian towns boast – sometimes truthfully as well – of having once been rich and powerful.

Little Ravello was indeed once a power to be reckoned with. The magnificence of the local cathedral of San Pantaleone testifies to that. The splendid 12th century bronze door with moving scenes of Christ's life, death and resurrection was shipped around the coast of Italy from Trani on the Adriatic – a heroic and costly enterprise. Study them for half an hour as I did as a cultural aperitif before lunch on yet another terrace; this time at the Villa Maria, a charming, low-key hotel with excellent food.

The specialties here are crespolini (crepes stuffed with sheep's milk ricotta) and soffiatini (crepes stuffed with

A tempting plate of seafood in Positano

spinach). Why crepes in Ravello? Il padrone of the Villa Maria, Vincenzo Palumbo, explained that crepes were popularised here about 50 years ago by a chef who had worked for the French owner of one of Ravello's many glamorous, if slightly forbidding, villas.

These villas of Ravello still house an international crowd, the most famous of whom is the American novelist Gore Vidal. Over lunch at the Villa Maria, Gore Vidal told me that he had been to a well-known restaurant and found that all the 'fresh, local' fish were either frozen or imported from abroad. Italy is a gastronomic paradise for me and many others, but it would be foolish to pretend that there wasn't occasionally trouble in paradise.

Later that afternoon Vincenzo took me to visit a friend's lemon grove to look at the famous Sfusato Amalfitana, 'the best lemons in the world'. They are huge and succulent and many end up in the local drink, lemoncello, a fantastically powerful mix of alcohol, sugar and lemon juice. I diplomatically sipped a thimbleful and said that it was just the nicest liqueur I'd ever drunk anywhere.

From Ravello we travelled inland along a road studded with threatening signs admonishing us to watch out for falling rocks, snow, ice and fog. Just as my nerves were about to be terminally frayed, we turned a corner and a vast plain was spread out before us. The volcanic ash and rock from nearby Mount Vesuvius had settled here to create a fantastically fertile region. The roadsides are punctuated by farmers' stands piled high with chillies, lemons, peaches and San Marzano tomatoes.

It is, of course, hard to think about Italian cooking without tomatoes, but they were only introduced to Italy and the rest of Europe in the 16th century. They first began to be used in cooking about 200 years later, although it wasn't until the late 19th century that the industrial tinning of tomatoes, really popularised them. The volcanic soils around Naples were ideal for producing big yields of sweet, juicy tomatoes and the plum-shaped tomatoes of San Marzano make their way all over the world in tins. The ten-hectare farm I visited, grew about a quarter of a million pounds of tomatoes a year as well as the beloved red chillies which flourished in polythene tunnels, where the temperature climbed up to 50 degrees centigrade at mid-day.

Signora Dora Longobardi, a farmer's wife, showed me how to make tomato sauce 'the way that real people from the Campania do on the farm'. She very finely chopped one clove of garlic and a small onion, and cooked them in olive oil for a couple of minutes. She added two kilograms of chopped, peeled tomatoes, a little bit of dried red chilli and some salt. She simmered the sauce for about 20 minutes and then just before serving threw in a generous handful of some of the biggest, greenest, roughest, most aromatic basil I've ever come across. The sauce went on to the spaghetti and it was dished up for us and the family without any grated cheese – 'no, never, never' – but with many bottles of rather basic red wine.

The sun slipped behind Vesuvius and we set off for Naples. As we dodged lorry loads of tomatoes on the motorway, I thought of the old travel slogan 'see Naples and die'.

LINGUINE 'VECCHIA TRANI'
Linguine 'Vecchia Trani'

90ml (6 tbsp) olive oil
2 cloves garlic, chopped
225g (8 oz) clams, scrubbed
225g (8 oz) mussels, scrubbed
100g (4 oz) canned cannellini beans
4 bay leaves
15ml (1 tbsp) fresh basil, chopped
2 fresh tomatoes, peeled and chopped
pinch of salt
500g (18 oz) linguine
parsley for garnish

SERVES 4

Cook the pasta for about 10 minutes or until *al dente*.
Meanwhile, heat the olive oil in a shallow frying pan and
fry the garlic. When the garlic is translucent, add the shell-
fish and cook until the shells have opened. Then add the
bay leaves, basil, tomatoes and salt and cook for 1 minute.
Remove from the heat.

Drain the pasta thoroughly and mix with the sauce in
the pan over a low heat for a few minutes.

Turn into a serving dish and garnish with parsley.

VERMICELLI WITH COURGETTES
Vermicelli con Gli Zucchini

This recipe is based on a secret creation of a trattoria on the Sorrento coast, and is most certainly not identical! The owner of the trattoria closely guards the original recipe, so the following is only our best guess at the components of this delicious dish. Two versions of this recipe exist: one using sweet Sorrento provolone, and the other using Romano cheese.

150ml (¼ pint) olive oil for frying
1kg (2¼ lb) medium-sized courgettes
100g (4 oz) Parmesan cheese, grated
100g (4 oz) sweet provolone cheese
50g (2 oz) butter
30ml (2 tbsp) fresh basil
salt and freshly ground black pepper
500g (18 oz) vermicelli

SERVES 6 - 8

Heat the oil in a deep frying pan. Cut the courgettes into thin slices and fry a few at a time in the hot oil, until the courgettes are browned. Remove the cooked courgettes from the frying pan and place in a large bowl with the two cheeses, the basil, butter and a little salt and pepper.

Cook the vermicelli until *al dente*, drain thoroughly and return to the saucepan in which it was cooked, together with the courgette mixture. If necessary, add a few spoonfuls of oil left over from frying the courgettes. Mix well over a very low heat and serve immediately.

RAVIOLI DONNA AMELIA
Ravioli Donna Amelia

For the sauce
60ml (4 tbsp) olive oil
500g (18 oz) pork, cut into small pieces
500g (18 oz) lean beef, cut into small pieces
25g (1 oz) raisins
15g ($^1/_2$ oz) pine nuts
1.4kg (3 lb) tomatoes, peeled and chopped
a pinch of salt
For the stuffing
500g (18 oz) mozzarella cheese, preferably buffalo
2 egg yolks, beaten
100g (4 oz) Parmesan cheese, freshly grated
For the pasta
400g (14 oz) plain flour
a pinch of salt
50g (2 oz) butter or white vegetable fat
1 egg
grated Parmesan cheese

SERVES 8 - 10

To make the sauce, heat the oil in a large pan and sauté the meat. Add the raisins, pine nuts, tomatoes and salt. Cook for 3 hours over a low heat, then remove the meat and blend the sauce in a food processor to ensure a smooth consistency.

For the stuffing, cut the mozzarella into small pieces and mix it with the egg yolk and Parmesan cheese. Set aside.

To make the pasta, sift the flour and salt directly on to a work surface, preferably marble. Mix the fat with a little hot water until a creamy consistency is achieved, then add the egg, and knead with the flour briefly to make a smooth dough. Roll out the pasta thinly and divide it into two sheets of equal size. Spread the stuffing on top of one sheet. Cover this with the other sheet, press the pasta around the filling to seal, then using a 2.5cm (1 inch) round pastry cutter, cut out the ravioli. Cook in boiling water for about 5 minutes and drain immediately. Do *not* rinse. Place in a serving dish.

Pour the sauce over the ravioli, sprinkle with Parmesan and serve immediately.

ARTICHOKES WITH MOZZARELLA CHEESE
Carciofi con Mozzarella

12 small globe artichokes
flour
lemon juice
salt and freshly ground black pepper
225g (8 oz) fresh mozzarella cheese, preferably buffalo, chopped
about 30ml (2 tbsp) chopped parsley
1 large egg, beaten
30ml (2 tbsp) grated Parmesan cheese
soft breadcrumbs
2 salted sardines
about 150ml (¼ pint) olive oil

SERVES 6

Trim the artichokes and discard the stems. Make a thin paste with flour, water and a little lemon juice. Then soak the artichokes in the paste for 30 minutes. Rinse in cold water, drain and dry them.

Open the tops of the artichokes and season lightly with salt. Blend the mozzarella cheese, parsley, egg, Parmesan cheese, salt and pepper together thoroughly. Stuff the artichokes with this mixture. Sprinkle a few breadcrumbs on top and add a small piece of sardine. Arrange the artichokes in a round pan in a circle. Pour a little oil over each one and then pour 125ml (4 fl oz) of water into the middle of the pan. Cook for about 30 minutes over a medium heat, adding a little water if necessary. Definitely add a little water 5 minutes before turning off the heat. Serve hot.

Peppers and figs, drying in the Italian sunshine

GROUPER BAKED IN TOMATO SAUCE
Cernia alla Marinara

The amount of sauce needed depends on the size of the fish. There should be sufficient sauce to cover it. This sauce is also excellent served with pasta.

about 700g (1½ lb) grouper, sea bass, flounder or other white fish

For the sauce
2 cloves garlic, chopped
450g (1 lb) tomatoes, peeled and coarsely chopped
45ml (3 tbsp) olive oil
15ml (1 tbsp) oregano, chopped
15ml (1 tbsp) parsley, chopped
salt and freshly ground black pepper

SERVES 4

Place the cleaned and filleted fish in an ovenproof dish. Combine the ingredients for the sauce and use to cover the fish. Cook in the oven at 180°C (350°F) mark 4 for about 20 minutes until fish is flaky.

SPAGHETTI WITH CLAMS
Spaghetti alle Vongole

You should always check on the label that the spaghetti is made with durum wheat.
Do not use fresh spaghetti in this recipe.

1kg (2¼ lb) clams
salt
500g (18 oz) spaghetti
2 cloves garlic, chopped
125ml (4 fl oz) extra virgin olive oil
45ml (3 tbsp) chopped parsley
2 dried red chilli peppers, finely chopped

SERVES 6

Cover the clams with salt water and leave for at least 30 minutes (longer if possible) to clean them.

Measure 2.5 litres (4½ pints) water into a large saucepan and bring to the boil. Add the pasta and a pinch of salt, stirring constantly until the water reaches boiling point again. When the pasta is *al dente*, drain thoroughly but do *not* rinse.

Put the garlic and oil in a large frying pan over a moderate heat. Add the cleaned clams with the parsley and dried red chilli pepper. Cook for about 5 minutes, until all the clams are open, discarding any that are still closed, and serve hot with the pasta.

WHISPERS
Soffiatini

For the filling
75g (3 oz) butter
75g (3 oz) plain flour
200ml (7 fl oz) milk
100g (4 oz) cooked spinach, shredded
a pinch of salt
100g (4 oz) mozzarella cheese, diced
75g (3 oz) Parma ham, shredded
50g (2 oz) Parmesan cheese, grated
a pinch of freshly ground black pepper
2 egg whites, whisked

For the pancakes
90g (3½ oz) plain flour
150ml (¼ pint) milk
2 eggs, beaten
a pinch of salt
a little melted butter
grated Parmesan cheese

SERVES 4

To make the filling, melt the butter in a saucepan, add the flour and cook for 1 minute to make a roux. Remove from the heat and leave to cool. Bring the milk to the boil, add to the roux and cook over a moderate heat until the sauce has thickened, stirring constantly. Add the spinach with a pinch of salt and cook for a further minute. Fold in the remaining ingredients and leave to cool.

To make the pancakes, mix the flour and milk in a saucepan, add the eggs with a pinch of salt and whip. Pass the batter through a sieve. Brush a 30cm (12 inch) diameter, heavy frying pan with melted butter and set over a moderate heat. Pour a small ladleful of the pancake batter into the pan and make a thin pancake. Repeat with the remaining batter.

When cooked on both sides, lay each pancake on a

plate. Put a spoonful of the filling in the centre of each pancake and fold over two edges to meet in the centre, then fold over the other two edges making a parcel. Place on a greased, high-sided baking tray. Brush with melted butter, sprinkle with Parmesan and bake in the oven at 180°C (350°F) mark 4 for 8-9 minutes.

CHOCOLATE ALMOND CAKE
Torta di Mandorle

200g (7 oz) butter
250g (9 oz) caster sugar
5 eggs, separated
200g (7 oz) semi-sweet chocolate, melted
250g (9 oz) almonds, finely chopped
grated rind of 1/2 lemon
sifted icing sugar

Melt the butter in the top of a double saucepan, then add the sugar and mix to a creamy consistency. Add the egg yolks and mix together. Then add the melted chocolate and almonds. Whisk the egg whites in a bowl until they form peaks, then add the grated lemon rind and mix gently with the chocolate mixture in a clockwise direction until completely blended.

Turn the mixture into a buttered and floured, 23cm (9 inch) round cake tin and bake in the oven at 190°C (375°F) mark 5 for 30-45 minutes, or until a skewer inserted into the centre comes out clean. Turn out on to a wire rack and leave at room temperature, then dust with icing sugar.

Naples to Torre de Lupara

In classical mythology the sirens were beautiful maidens who used music to lure sailors to their deaths. One of the sirens, Parthenope, was drowned and her body was washed up on the Italian coast, on the site where the city of Naples was later built. Naples, Parthenope's city, is like the siren herself – seductive and dangerous.

Naples is a hard city to get to grips with, hence its fascination. It is the Manhattan of the Med, the Africa of Italy, a place of immense sophistication and charm, as well as off-putting degrees of crime, heat, dirt and squalor. Tourists are urged to be wary of gangs of motorscooter-riding youths who may be attracted by visiting cameras, handbags and wristwatches. On this visit, the city administration was in a state of financial collapse, so basic urban services were grinding to a halt. All the traffic lights in town were out and the city was trapped in a boiling ill-tempered gridlock.

Naples is blessed with one of the most ravishing settings of any city in the world. The intensely blue Bay of Naples, and the still-threatening hulk of Vesuvius, are the physical anchors of Neapolitan life. The often crumbling, but undeniably grand, architecture reflects Naples' historical power and cultural pre-eminence – it was an obligatory stop on the European grand tour for 18th century British nobs. Modern visitors will still be dazzled by the acoustics of the San Carlo Opera House and the treasures of the National Archeological Museum.

The cookery of Naples has always been remarked upon by travellers. In the late 17th century John Ray, an English traveller, noted: 'macarones and vermicelle which are nothing but a kind of paste, cut into the figure of worms... boil'd in broth or water are a great dish here'. Pasta was a staple of the poor that also figured in the elaborate and sometimes

A traditional pizza being prepared in Naples

rather theatrical dishes that the luxury-loving Neapolitan aristocracy ate. Thanks to successive invasions by Byzantines, Goths, Lombards, Normans, Spaniards and even Austrians, the cuisine of Naples can be complex and exotic.

In the mid-19th century, the Duke of Buonvicino attempted to codify the cooking of his native city in his heroic cookbook, *Theory and Practice of Cooking according to the Four Seasons*. When a duke writes a cookbook, you know that you're dealing with a society that takes eating seriously. At the time that Buonvicino wrote the book, pizza was still a local product that had yet to conquer the world.

How old is pizza? No one knows, but there is something that looks like a vulcanised pizza excavated from the ruins of Pompeii. Certainly pizza has been eaten in Naples for centuries. But it took a royal PR stunt to catapult pizza from the back streets of Naples to global fame. On July 11th, 1889, Queen Margherita of Italy, wife of King Umberto I, was in Naples on a state visit. She was taken to a little back-street pizzeria where Raffaele Esposito presented her with a pizza he had baked specially for the state visit – white mozzarella, red tomatoes and green basil leaves flavoured the pizza and made up the colours of the Italian flag. The Queen tasted the patriotic pizza and approved.

Esposito married the boss's daughter and inherited the Pizzeria Brandi which still flourishes. A commemorative tablet was put up in 1989 announcing that 'Here One Hundred Years Ago the Pizza Margherita was Born'. The walls of the tiny pizzeria are plastered with press cuttings. A typical headline reads 'The Queen tasted the pizza and called it regal', and there are numerous photographs of the current proprietor, Vincenzo Pagnano, sharing a pizza with presidents, prime ministers, film stars and celebrated intellectuals. You can in fact order something new fangled like a smoked salmon pizza, but most people will come here for one of the classics, perhaps the mother of all pizzas, the marinara, which is frugally topped with tomatoes, garlic and oregano.

Unsurprisingly, everyone in Naples has a different and violently held opinion about the best pizza in town, but they all agree that Naples is the only place to eat pizza. 'Anywhere in Naples you can eat excellent pizza,' Vincenzo tells me, 'but by the time you get as far as Sorrento, which is only 50 kilometres away, the pizzas are horrible.' At Brandi, the pizza dough is flour, water, a little salt, beer yeast and some of the leftover dough from the day before. Some pizzerias add a bit of strutto, or pig fat, which they claim produces a more delicate pizza.

At Brandi and every other proper pizzeria, the pizzas are cooked in a wood-fired oven. The wood – often oak – smoke adds to the flavour and perhaps more importantly the intense heat which climbs to around 450 degrees centigrade allows for a crisp crust and a short cooking time (just a few minutes). In general, the further south in Italy the thinner the crust. The pizza makers, or pizzaioli, of Naples are prized specialists who work their ingredients vigorously, but you will rarely see them tossing dough up in the air. 'That's so American,' Vincenzo remarks, 'they should be performing in a circus not in a pizzeria.'

Recently a British supermarket began selling a frozen pizza that it claimed was made from Brandi's recipe. Vincenzo had tried it. What was it like? 'Fa schiff!' he barks in Neapolitan dialect, a reply which I can only politely translate as 'It sucks'.

In Naples, pizza is eaten mostly at night, always bought from a pizzeria and never cooked at home. You wash it down with wine or, increasingly, with beer, a habit introduced by the American GIs who occupied Naples at the end of the last war. Pizza is a famous but small part of the culinary landscape. In Naples, eating well is part of everyone's life. A Neapolitan friend told me that as a small child in the 1930s he was taken to look at one of the restaurants in the borgo marinaro, at the little fisherman's port of Santa Lucia, at the foot of Naples' romantic Egg Castle (Castel dell' Ovo). 'Look at those poor people,' my friend's mother then said, pointing to the relatively rich diners inside the restaurant, 'they can't eat well enough at home so they have to come to places like this!' As in many other parts of Italy, home is where the real cooking is found.

A stroll up the steep narrow street where the Pizzeria Brandi is located took me past dozens of enthralling food shops. One window was piled high with freselle bread, which is made with flour, salt and yeast, and then dried for storage and soaked in water to be rubbed with garlic, and topped with tomatoes or to be served alongside big bowls of tripe stew. My favourite shop had a facade inlaid with hundreds of seashells and a handwritten sign proclaiming 'Questo vongolaio e piu famoso nel mondo,' which means 'These clams are' – you guessed it – 'the best in the world'.

Alongside the wooden trays of clams were mussels, octopus and grey mullet. Astonishingly some of the fish sold in Naples is still caught right in the bay. Whatever time of day or night I looked out of my hotel window, there was an industrious, or perhaps just optimistic, fisherman laying out his nets against the background of the commercial shipping traffic of the Bay of Naples. The whole bay of Naples is fringed with little restaurants where you can eat

Pizza Margherita at the Pizzeria Brandi

spaghetti alle vongole, naturally, or a fritto misto (a plate of mixed fried fish). Some of these places are quite good, others have, not unexpectedly, degenerated into mere tourist traps peddling mediocre food in an irresistibly 'authentic' setting.

Some travellers will tell you that picturesque Santa Lucia or Posillipo, the upmarket seafront suburb to the north, isn't the real Naples, but they're just there for tourists. Well, much of Naples has been 'just for tourists' for hundreds of years and isn't any less 'real' for all of that.

Our search for a different type of pizza took us into some neighbourhoods that were certainly off the tourist agenda. If the pizza has become familiar to the residents of Topeka and Tokyo, the pizza fritti has stayed resolutely

Children in the streets of Naples enjoy 'pizza on the hoof'

Neapolitan. In the dense residential quarters of the city where laundry hangs between the tall and narrow blocks of flats to make cool and dark streets, life is noisy and communal and the food of the streets is fried pizza.

Two elderly sisters, Antonietta Ferraro and Concetta Santilla, sell their much-praised fried pizza from an open-fronted shop. There are a few tables inside but pizza fritti, like fish and chips, is meant to be wrapped in paper and eaten on the hoof. The simple dough – flour, water, salt, a little leavening – is stuffed full of salami, mozzarella, ricotta and tomatoes and plunged into a tank of boiling oil. The result – a fat, golden turnover that ain't exactly delicate – is to my palate an acquired taste, but it appears to keep most of the population of Naples well fuelled.

White, milky and slightly bland mozzarella cheese is hard to get away from in Naples. Most people are familiar with mozzarella as a pizza topping or part of an insalata caprese (mozzarella, tomato and basil salad) named in tribute to the beautiful island of Capri, a short hop across the bay from Naples. Indeed, the cheese turns up in dozens of dishes throughout the varied Neapolitan culinary repertoire.

You can buy bricks of Danish-made mozzarella in British supermarkets if all you want is white, rubbery cheese. But if you want to taste what mozzarella is really all about you have to seek out mozzarella di bufala, which is made from the milk of water buffaloes. The animals were introduced from India sometime during the Middle Ages, perhaps even as early as the eighth century: they had the endurance and disease resistance to work the malaria-infested marshlands of the south.

We visited the largest buffalo herd in the country at the Torre de Lupara dairy built around a cluster of ancient farm buildings. There are 1,600 of these handsome and hardy beasts in the herd, each bearing a little yellow identity tag in their left ear. My girlfriend was number 4599, an affectionate half-ton buffalo who produces about 60 litres of buffalo milk a day. Whenever 4599 gave me an affectionate nuzzle, it was a bit like being run down by a Chieftain tank.

Buffalo milk is fat, but mild, yielding about one kilogram of cheese for every four litres of milk. (You need about 12 litres of cows' milk to produce one kilogram of cheese.) The cheese ought to be eaten as simply and freshly as possible. At lunch with the Jemma family who own the herd, I ran through a gamut of mozzarella dishes, but nothing tasted better than the simplest: cheese made that morning with a light drizzle of olive oil. The little football-shaped cheeses shouldn't be sliced the way they serve them in restaurants, one of the Jemma sons explained. He carefully cut the mozzarella into quarters: that way you get just the right amount of slightly salty outside to balance the sweeter flavour of the inner cheese.

After lunch I went back out into the fields to say 'arrivederci' to 4599 who responded with a slimy lick with her rough, black, labrador-sized tongue. We drove off into the hills of Umbria, passing through miles of tobacco fields, most of whose produce finds its way into counterfeit packs of cigarettes which itinerant peddlers sell by motorway tollgates. We passed on the cigarettes, but bought some counterfeit cassettes instead. Southern Italy has its own laws.

MOZZARELLA IN A CARRIAGE
Mozzarella in Carrozza

300g (11 oz) mozzarella cheese
8 small slices of bread
150g (5 oz) cooked ham, cut into 4 slices
salt and freshly ground black pepper
90ml (6 tbsp) milk
15ml (1 tbsp) plain flour
1 egg, beaten
60ml (4 tbsp) oil for frying

Lay a slice of mozzarella cheese on four slices of the bread.
Cover with the cooked ham, season with salt and pepper and cover with the remaining slices of bread.
Pass each sandwich through the milk, then in the flour and finally in the beaten egg. Heat the oil in a frying pan. Add the sandwiches and fry until golden brown, turning once. Serve immediately.

QUESTO
VONGOLAIO
E PIU
FAMOSO NEL
MONDO
QUESTO
VONGOLAIO
È IL
N. 1 LA

SPAGHETTI CAPRI-STYLE
Spaghetti alla Caprese

250g (9 oz) cherry tomatoes
45ml (3 tbsp) olive oil
1 clove garlic, chopped
500g (18 oz) spaghetti
salt
200g (7 oz) mozzarella cheese
chopped fresh basil
chopped fresh oregano

SERVES 4

Cut the cherry tomatoes into small, chunky pieces. Put in a dish with the oil and garlic and marinate for 30 minutes.

Meanwhile cook the spaghetti in plenty of boiling water until *al dente*. Add the mozzarella cheese to the marinade. Drain the spaghetti thoroughly and mix with the marinade. Sprinkle with basil and oregano.

Opposite: Clams on sale in Naples

Below: It takes just 4 litres of water buffaloes' milk to make a kilogram of delicious mozzarella

AUBERGINE ROLLS WITH MOZZARELLA CHEESE
Melanzane arrotolate con Mozzarella

1 kg (2½ lb) aubergine
oil for frying
300g (11 oz) mozzarella cheese
grated Parmesan cheese
cooked tomato (optional)
fresh basil (optional)

SERVES 6 - 8

Cut the aubergine lengthwise into slices about 5mm (¼ inch) thick. Heat the oil in a frying pan and fry the slices of aubergine until soft and tender. Drain on paper towels.

Put a piece of mozzarella cheese and a little grated Parmesan cheese on each slice of aubergine. Roll each one up carefully and put in a roasting tin. Add a little cooked tomato and basil if liked. Cook in the oven at 190°C (375°F) mark 5 for about 10 minutes.

MOZZARELLA AND TOMATO FANS
Ventagli di Pomodoro con Mozzarella

4 large tomatoes (not very ripe)
salt and freshly ground black pepper
225g (8 oz) mozzarella cheese
lettuce leaves
2 carrots, cut into julienne

SERVES 4

Wash and dry the tomatoes. Cut them in even slices, taking care not to cut right through the base of the tomato. Season lightly with salt and pepper. Insert a matching slice of mozzarella cheese between each slice of tomato to make a fan shape. Place each fan on a lettuce leaf and garnish with carrot.

NAPLES – TORRE DE LUPARA

NEAPOLITAN TIMBALE OF PASTA
Timballo di Ziti 'Vecchia Napoli'

200ml (7 fl oz) olive oil
500g (18 oz) fillet pork, thickly sliced
1kg (2¼ lb) ham bones
2 carrots, chopped
100g (4 oz) onion, chopped
4 sticks celery, chopped
1kg (2 lb) tomatoes, peeled and chopped
500ml (18 fl oz) passata (creamed tomatoes)
200g (7 oz) Italian sausages, sliced
200ml (7 fl oz) red wine
200g (7 oz) peas, cooked
500g (18 oz) ziti pasta, boiled and drained
100g (4 oz) Parmesan cheese, grated
450g (1 lb) short crust pastry
200g (7 oz) mozzarella cheese, chopped
3 hard-boiled eggs, sliced
1 egg, beaten

SERVES 10

Heat 175ml (6 fl oz) of the oil in a large saucepan. Brown the pork and add the ham bones, carrots, half the onion, celery, tomatoes and passata. Simmer for about 2 hours to make a rich sauce. Discard the ham bones.

Remove the cooked pork and dice it. Heat the remaining oil in a shallow pan and brown the remaining onion. Add the pork and sausages. Pour over the red wine and reduce over a moderate heat. Then add a little of the sauce, bring to the boil and add the peas. Add the cooked pasta and three-quarters of the Parmesan cheese and mix well. Meanwhile, simmer the reserved sauce for 20 minutes, then leave to cool.

Roll out the pastry and use half to line a large pie dish. Spread the mozzarella, egg slices and the remaining Parmesan over the base, then add the pasta mixture. Cover with the remaining pastry. Brush the top with beaten egg and bake in the oven at 200°C (400°F) mark 6 for 20 minutes, or until cooked. Cool and serve in slices with the sauce.

Signore Battilochi with truffles, the objects of his devotion

From Norcia to Spoleto

A mock coat of arms hangs on the wall above us inscribed 'Republica del tartufo – Vittorio da Norcia'. We are momentarily in the Republic of Truffles, under the benign, rotund aegis of Vittorio Battilochi, an Umbrian restaurateur whose establishment in the ancient hill town of Norcia is a place of pilgrimage and celebration for truffle lovers.

Battilochi's menu offers an A to Z of truffle cookery beginning with the Z – zuppa di porcini e tartufi (wild mushroom and truffle soup) and progressing through some two dozen dishes to truffle ice cream. Even by the standards of truffle-mad Norcia, Signor Battilochi's devotion to the tuber is extraordinary, and his restaurant is crowded with studious American visitors, bemused French,

Truffles in close-up

hungry Italians, and a superstar chef from Japan who is here for a crash course on truffle cooking. If you have never seen, smelled or tasted truffles – and most people haven't – you might not understand what the fuss is all about. Truffles are among the most highly priced, hard-to-find and difficult-to-appreciate foods in the world. They also attract a disproportionate amount of mystique and snobbery. Like many other expensive and arcane foods, they are meant to be an aphrodisiac. They are a fungus that grows underground, close to certain trees like oak, chestnut or poplar. Of many different varieties, the two most famous are the *Tuber magnatum* (white truffle) and the *Tuber melanosporum* (black truffle). In Italy white truffle production is centred around Alba in the Piedmont, up in the north-west, while the black truffle capital is right here in Norcia.

As you would expect by now, partisans of the white truffle dismiss the black truffle as bland, ugly and useless; supporters of the black truffle think that the white truffle is vulgar, pretentious and coarse. The most distinctive aspect of all truffles is their smell, a smell that may be described poetically, as the novelist Thackeray did when he wrote about 'something musky, fiery, savoury, mysterious – a hot drowsy smell that lulls the senses and yet enflames them'. More down-to-earth truffle lovers may candidly admit that you only have to think of old socks. And by their smell shall they be found. Because they grow underground, the only way to find a truffle is to sniff them out and the sniffing is done by trained pigs, or dogs.

I met a local truffle hunter on a hill about five miles outside of Norcia. He parked his old battered Fiat at our rendezvous point and climbed out, dressed from head to toe in early Rambo-style camouflage. 'Where's the dog?' I asked. He opened the boot of his car and a beautiful springer spaniel, called Boccanera, leapt out. The dog was four years old and had had ten months of intensive training before going out into the woods for serious truffle hunting. During the hunting season, the dogs are kept rather hungry to increase their keenness: poor Boccanera had only eaten a little bread that day. But he was in a state of great excitement as we set off into the woods. He sniffed carefully around the tree trunks and then began digging furiously. His master called him off and finished the work with a truffle-hunting spade. At the end of an afternoon's hunt, Boccanera had found a handful of truffles: they looked like misshapen, dirt-encrusted golf balls.

Even in Norcia the best truffles can sell for anything up to one million lire a kilogram (about £250 a pound). In spite of the price, visitors to Norcia eat truffles profligately. At the restaurant we ate smoked turkey breast with truffles, tortellini with truffles, and beef with truffle sauce. Pudding was chocolate ice cream with – I'm not joking – truffles. The flavours of earth and chocolate blended together surprisingly well. The Nursini, as the inhabitants of the town are called, eat truffles with rather less abandon: long experience has taught them that a little truffle goes a long way.

Norcia itself is one of the most enchanting places in Italy. It is tucked away in the mountainous eastern corner of Umbria, and you approach through wild landscape and winding roads. You enter the town through a triumphal gateway with Latin inscriptions. The centrepiece of the place is the Piazza San Benedetto, a miniature square with a grandeur that puts it up alongside the Place de la Concorde and St. Mark's Square. The Piazza is framed by a big church, the town hall, and a charming fortified palace built in the mid-16th century by the celebrated Renaissance architect Vignola for the indolent and luxurious Pope Julius III. In the crypt of the church you can visit the sketchily preserved remains of the Roman house where Norcia's most famous son, Saint Benedict, and his twin sister, Saint Scholastica, were born in the fifth century. Benedict became the father of Western monasticism, and he is also honoured as the patron of Europe. Enough culture.

The square is also, like everywhere else in Norcia, home to a pig butcher's shop. The truffle is, to use a religious analogy, just one element of the gastronomic trinity here,

A 'Norcheria' in Norcia

the others being the pig and the lentil. Pigs first. The acorns and chestnuts of the forests are ideal fodder for local pigs, and the pig butchers of Norcia have been celebrated for centuries so much that a 'Norceria' is a common term for a pig butcher's all over Italy. Here the butcher's shops are palaces of piggery. Exteriors are extravagantly decorated with boars' heads; inside the rafters bend under the weight of hams and salamis.

You will also find huge barrels of dried chick peas, canellini beans and a selection of the best lentils. You will know about red lentils, which tend to pop up in Indian cooking as dhal, and green lentils, which are classically served in pork dishes in France. Here there are the lentils of Castellucio, which are five times more expensive than

Out for a day's truffling in the Italian countryside

any other lentils on the market and well worth it. Tiny and beautiful, they range from dark brown to pale green, with the odd flash of orange. They are cultivated on the remarkable landscape of the Piano Grande, a huge flat meadow amongst the wild Umbrian mountains.

One evening we dined in an atmosphere-laden dining room at the Hotel de la Posta where the owner Sergio Bianconi presented a succession of Umbrian dishes, kicking off with an absolutely ravishing crostino of lentils (a thick chunk of toast topped with a big ladleful of stewed Casteluccio lentils). Then there was a heroic plateful of parpadelle alla Norcina. These broad, flat noodles are dished up with a rich sauce of sausages broken up and cooked in butter, with cream and parmigiano added towards the end. Just before serving, some truffle is grated over each helping. At the end of the meal we drank to the health of Norcia with glasses of the local truffle-flavoured grappa. Alas it wasn't really for me: I could only think of compost flavoured cough mixture.

The journey to Spoleto through the mountains, is short and breathtaking. Spoleto is much bigger than Norcia and more definitely on the international tourist map, since the Italo-American composer Giancarlo Menotti established the Festival of the Two Worlds there nearly 40 years ago. Like Norcia it was a Roman city (Spoletium) and tough enough to turn back Hannibal and his elephants on their way to Rome. In the Middle Ages, Spoleto became part of the Papal States and there was a brief interlude when Lucrezia Borgia was first lady of the city. Today it is inevitably full of tourists, but its remarkable churches – especially the pure and rigorous beauty of the 12th century Sant'Eufemia, a Romanesque church par excellence – and civic architecture are thankfully unspoiled.

There are good restaurants, too, where you can eat classic Umbrian dishes that use the game and herbs of this wild and remote region so deliciously. We ate amazingly well at the rather musically themed *Le Pentegramma*, where they took us into the kitchen to watch strangozzi being made. Strangozzi, served up with tomato and herb sauce or wild asparagus, or unsurprisingly with truffles, is a very different sort of fresh pasta because it is made without eggs. The herb and tomato sauce was just ravishing, largely because they cooked it very, very quickly indeed, to preserve the lovely fresh tomato taste, and also because they used far more herbs – great handfuls of basil and thyme – more lavishly than you would be advised in recipe books. One thing that doesn't exist in good cooking anywhere in Italy is timidity. The two women in the kitchen here went at their strangozzi like a team of SAS hit men: the result was big and bold. Afterwards a plate of sausages cooked with grapes made a sharp and refreshing contrast. It was our first truffle-free meal for days!

POACHER'S TROUT
Trota alla Bracconiera

4 trout, about 250g (9 oz) each
salt
flour
10 juniper berries
rapeseed or sunflower oil for frying
50g (2 oz) butter
30ml (2 tbsp) white wine
juice of $1/2$ lemon

SERVES 4

Clean and wash the trout, then season with salt and coat in flour. Crush five of the juniper berries and divide between the cavities.

Heat the oil in a frying pan and fry the trout until they are golden on both sides. Remove the fish from the pan. Fry the remaining juniper berries in the oil, then drain off the oil, add the butter, wine and lemon juice and cook slowly over a low heat until it turns brown. Serve immediately.

SAUSAGES WITH GRAPES
Salsicce all'Uva

This dish is traditionally made at grape harvest time.

allow 2 pork sausages per person
oil for frying
grapes

Prick the sausages all over with a fork and brown them in a frying pan with a little oil and some water – the quantity depends on the number of sausages. When the water has evaporated, add as many grapes as you like to the sausages. Cook for about 20 minutes, stirring often, and serve piping hot.

FETTUCINI SPOLETO-STYLE
Strangozzi di Spoleto

Proverb! 'What goes into your mouth doesn't harm you, it's what escapes from it.' The peculiarity of these home-made fettucini is that they do not contain any egg.

600g (1¹/₄ lb) plain flour
2 cloves garlic
60ml (4 tbsp) oil
1kg (2¹/₄ lb) ripe tomatoes, peeled and chopped
30-45ml (2-3 tbsp) fresh basil
salt and freshly ground black pepper

SERVES 6

Knead the flour with as much water as is needed to form a smooth dough. Roll out thinly and cut into strips about 1 cm (¹/₂ inch) wide. Leave to dry for several hours.

Heat the oil in a large saucepan and fry the garlic cloves. When they are brown, remove them from the pan and add the tomatoes with plenty of basil. Season with salt and pepper. Reduce the sauce by simmering for about 30

Strangozzi - delicious home-made fettucini

minutes.Cook the fettucini in plenty of boiling water until it is *al dente* (one of the secrets for success in this recipe). Drain and serve immediately with the sauce and grated Parmesan if liked.

ANCHOVY AND VINEGAR SALAD DRESSING
Acciughe in Salsa di Olio e Aceto

1 anchovy
45ml (3 tbsp) wine vinegar
125ml (4 fl oz) olive oil
salt

Cut the anchovy into small pieces. Heat a little oil in a frying pan and cook the anchovy until it is completely softened. Make a vinaigrette with the vinegar, anchovy, oil and salt.

Use to dress lettuce leaves.

TRUFFLE FRASCARELLI
Frascarelli Tartufati

500g (18 oz) plain flour
4 eggs
oil
1 small onion, finely chopped
45ml (3 tbsp) fresh basil
1 slice ham, finely chopped
60ml (4 tbsp) chopped tomatoes
1 stick celery, finely chopped
salt and freshly ground black pepper
truffle oil
slivers of black truffles from Norcia

SERVES 4

Put the flour into a bowl, make a well in the centre and break in the eggs. Mix together with your hands and rub until you obtain flakes about the size of coffee beans. These are called *frascarelli* in Italian.

Heat a little oil in a frying pan and fry the onion and herbs. Add the ham to the pan and brown it.

Add the tomatoes and celery, with enough water for the mixture to be served to four people.

Season with salt and pepper. Bring the mixture to the boil and simmer for 30 minutes. Add the *frascarelli,* stirring constantly so that the mixture does not become lumpy. Cook for about 7 minutes.

Serve in cups with a drop of truffle oil and a few slivers of black truffle.

MINESTRONE WITH SPELT
Minestra di Farro

Spelt is a type of wheat which is pounded in a pestle and mortar. This does not grind it but merely breaks it into little lumps. It is available in health food shops which sell a wide range of grains.

1 ham bone, well scraped
200g (7 oz) ripe tomatoes, chopped
1 carrot, chopped
2 sticks celery, chopped
1 onion, chopped
300g (11 oz) spelt or bulgar wheat
grated Pecorino cheese, to serve

SERVES 6

Rinse the ham bone in running cold water and then soak in tepid water for 4 - 5 hours.

Put the ham bone in a large saucepan, cover with cold water, bring to the boil and simmer for about 15 minutes. Drain and cover with fresh water. Add the vegetables and cook for a further 2 hours.

Strain the liquid and bring it to the boil in a clean saucepan. Add the spelt slowly, stirring constantly, and cook for a further 30 minutes.

Add small pieces of lean ham taken from the bone and serve the soup very hot with plenty of grated Pecorino cheese.

A shop window displays just a small selection of Italian salami and sausages

 Into Tuscany

After wild, holy and relatively unspoiled Umbria, I feared that my dear Tuscany might seem tame and betouristed: I nearly fell into the currently popular sport of 'Tuscany knocking'. It is a region of Italy long loved by English travellers. Indeed the part of Tuscany that we were approaching, is such an undisputed English favourite that some 'sophisticated' visitors sneeringly refer to it as 'Chiantishire'.

Among the reasons for Tuscany's enduring popularity might be an enchanting landscape that appears to be straight out of a 14th-century altarpiece, a sprinkling of picturesque castles in varying states of grandeur, or perhaps more culture per square mile than anywhere else in Europe. The roster of Tuscany's starring artists runs from Alberti, the founding father of the Renaissance, to Verrochio, painter and sculptor, who taught the young Leonardo a thing or two. For many people, Tuscany is the Italian idyll.

Tuscan food is increasingly – and really rather erroneously – seen as what Italian food should be. For many people whose first experience of Italian cooking is some sort of bastardised Neapolitan cuisine – remember that the impoverished south of Italy is a great exporter of people, who have taken their native cooking around the world. Tuscan food is lighter, simpler, healthier, more 'modern'. It is a type of cooking that has benefited hugely from the work of two inspired propagandists, Giuliano Bugialli and Lorenza de Medici, whose Tuscan-based cookbooks have been internationally influential.

Curiously, Tuscan food is dismissed by many Italians. There is a popular saying that in Tuscany they 'cuocere' (cook) whilst in the rest of Italy they 'cucinare' (make a cuisine). It is true that the cooking of Tuscany is rustic and uncomplicated; it is, in spite of Tuscan prosperity, a 'cucina povera', a style of cooking based on common ingredients. But they are common ingredients selected with care and prepared with devotion: it is a way of cooking that has a lot to teach us. Other Italians have nicknamed Tuscans 'mangafagioles' (bean eaters), which I assume pokes fun at their low gastronomic aspirations. But there is nowhere in the world – with the shining exception of my home town of Boston – where you will eat such ravishing beans as in Tuscany.

Just as Tuscany is not Italy, Chianti is not Tuscany. Before we come to the red wine, which is the area's most celebrated and sometimes notorious international ambassador, there is the land itself. Chianti is a hilly area of central Tuscany that has been well settled since Etruscan times. Because of its location between the powerful rival cities of Florence and Siena, the gentle, wooded slopes of Chianti were a battlefield throughout the Middle Ages, as Florentine and Sienese dominion over the area ebbed and flowed. The large number of castles, that dot the countryside, are a legacy of hundreds of years of vicious, sporadic intercity warfare. The descendants of the powerful medieval lords of the Chianti are still very much in evidence and some, like the Ricasoli, are known to millions, thanks to the areas most famous export, Chianti wine.

Wine has been made here since ancient times, but Chianti wine itself is a 19th century invention, fermented from a complex blend of grapes devised and codified by the remarkable Bettino Ricasoli. Nicknamed 'the iron baron', Ricasoli was the second Prime Minister of the newly united Italy. The Prime Minister's newly invented wine became a big success, helped greatly by its bottle – the round fiasco, or flask, wrapped in a woven straw covering. The fiasco was memorable and picturesque, an infallible sales gimmick. So infallible that even the filthiest wine could receive a powerful dash of romance and rustic charm once bottled in a fiasco. Some readers may remember the days when a fiasco of Chianti meant a small bill but a huge headache.

Chianti winemakers, keen to be taken seriously, abandoned their trademark fiasco with indecent haste in the sixties and seventies and began putting their wine into restrained claret-style bottles. As in other wine-making regions of Italy, standards rose and so did prices. Today, Chiantis are more than a cheap and cheerful drink, and a new breed of locally produced wines, nicknamed the Super Tuscans, are competing in the highest echelons of the wine world.

As you drive through Chianti now, you can't help but notice the amount of money that has been invested in the wine trade: gleaming tractors, artistic labels, wine tastings in designer tasting rooms. Lorenza de Medici's husband, Piero Stucchi-Prinetti, was among the first producers of the new breed of high class Chiantis. He and Lorenza have turned their estate of Badia a Coltibuono into an internationally recognised brand name. The very lucky few participate in one of Lorenza's cookery courses at the old Benedictine monastery, but many more people visit there to eat in the restaurant, or to buy a bottle or two of wine, or some of Badia's outstanding olive oil.

Tuscany is one of the great olive growing regions of Italy, and in recent years the same effort and investment that has gone into wine making has been directed towards the olive oil business. As we head further north we will enter the Italy of butter, where butter replaces olive oil as the principal cooking fat. But much of Italy, from Tuscany southwards, is just too mountainous to graze dairy cattle efficiently; the rocky landscape is much better suited to the cultivation of olives.

When olive oil is called for in any Italian recipe, you cannot and should not substitute any other oil. Olive oil has unique culinary properties that no other oil or blend of oil can begin to approach. You can buy perfectly decent blended olive oils or slightly better virgin olive oils in most British supermarkets, which will do more than adequately, for everyday cooking and salads, at a reasonable price. But if you want to experience the thrill of olive oil you will have to dig deep: you can spend £15 and more a bottle for

Above: *The author, with friends, in a quiet courtyard*

Opposite: Olive oil, the basis of so much Italian food

Below: *Fresh basil for sale*

the real thing – an extra virgin, estate-bottled oil from Tuscany. Lest you be confused by the terminology, virgin olive oil is oil produced by what could broadly be called traditional methods – in other words, no heating and no chemical shenanigans.

The best grade of oil, extra virgin, will have less than one per cent acidity. Sadly, many extra virgins are produced on a mass, industrial scale, and have little of the charm or character of the best oils. Your palate, a highish price and the advice of your local specialist shop should guide you. Olive oils are as different and as rewarding as great wines. Although I love the oils of Liguria in the north-west and Apulia in the south-east, Tuscan oils from Chianti are my favourite treat. Along with really excellent butter, a great oil is one of the few cooking fats that has a really sublime flavour. I don't want to enter the medical debate about good fats and bad fats, but it does seem that olive oil-based diets are good for you.

This digression about olive oil is very pertinent to most Italian, and particularly to most Tuscan, cooking. There is an American acronym, KISS, which stands for 'keep it simple, stupid'. Simplicity is the watchword for much of the best Italian cooking, but that simplicity must be complemented by an absolute devotion to finding and using the best possible ingredients. Do not settle for any old oil, tomato or tin of anchovies that you can lay your hands on. Go out and find the best!

Our base in Chianti was the Castello di Spaltenna, a castle that was pretty and romantic, even by the high, local standards. The castle itself is a medieval fortified monastery with a charming little Romanesque church punctuated by a huge square bell tower which stands alongside it like a limestone exclamation mark. The afternoon we arrived, a wedding was in progress; after the service the guests poured into the castle courtyard for their wedding feast. In the midst of all the festivities, Seamus, the chef and co-owner, appeared to help us with our bags. Yes, I did say Seamus, and if I said Seamus de Pentheny O'Kelly you would be even more certain that he wasn't an Italian.

Seamus is, dare I say, famously eccentric in Tuscany, and eccentric hoteliers in general give me the creeps. Just mention a man with a monocle or a handlebar moustache or a penchant for Victorian fancy dress and I'm checking into another hotel. I shall tell you that Seamus is an Irish South African, who trained with Paul Bocuse and is known to put on African tribal gear and play the bongos after dinner. He, and his partner Julia Scammozzi, have turned the sleepy hamlet of Spaltenna into a notable destination.

Paradoxically, in this area which is so rich with good food, there are few good local restaurants and Seamus' dining room is a great favourite with the local residents. He has studied classic Tuscan cookery and he brings a verve and unusual iconoclasm to the Italian kitchen. Many years ago, an Italian friend pulled me aside and whispered conspiratorially that he had seen one of our more well-known Italian chefs stirring a risotto with a metal spoon rather than a wooden one. 'How could he do such a thing?' he asked me in horror and despair. I thought about him as I stood in the kitchen at Spaltenna and watched Seamus cook the most astonishingly unorthodox risotto I have ever witnessed. When it came to the table, full of Swiss chard and purple onions, gently spiked with pungent nepitella (Tuscan wild mint), it turned out to be one of the most delicious risotti I have ever tasted.

Seamus has also memorably introduced some of the hot flavours of South Africa into normally mild-mannered Tuscan dishes. One of his specialities is a chilli-laden steak sandwich called a prego. 'Prego means a nail in Portuguese and this sauce just nails you to the wall. I've had Italian clients go crazy over it,' he laughs. His approach to this traditional cuisine makes him one of the most captivating subversives to be found in any Italian kitchen.

BEAN SOUP
Zuppa di Spattenna

300g (11 oz) haricot or cannellini beans
5ml (1 tsp) bicarbonate of soda
60ml (4 tbsp) olive oil
2 onions, roughly chopped
2 sticks celery, roughly chopped
2 carrots, roughly chopped
2 potatoes, roughly chopped
4 leaves of black cabbage, cut into small pieces
4 leaves of Savoy cabbage, cut into small pieces
2 - 3 slices of Parma ham
extra virgin olive oil

SERVES 4

Soak the beans overnight in cold water with the bicarbonate of soda. Rinse in fresh cold water and drain.

Heat the oil in a large saucepan and brown the onions, celery and carrots for 10 minutes. Add the remaining vegetables and cook for another 10 minutes. Add the beans and Parma ham to the vegetables, cover with water and Simmer for about 3 hours. Serve with a drop of extra virgin olive oil in each portion.

CEP PARCELS
Funghi Porcini al Cartoccio

A variety of wild mint called *nepitella* is used in Italy for this dish. Ceps are a type of mushroom with a smooth brown cap.

4 medium-sized ceps
60ml (4 tbsp) olive oil
4 garlic cloves, cut into slivers
4 small sprigs wild mint, or parsley, finely chopped
salt and freshly ground black pepper

SERVES 4

Wipe the mushrooms with a clean damp cloth. Cut off the stems and chop finely.

Brush four squares of foil liberally with the olive oil. Place a mushroom cap in the centre and divide the chopped stems equally between each square. Sprinkle with the garlic and herbs, add a little more oil and season with salt and pepper.

Bring the corners of each square of foil up to meet in the centre and fold over to seal the contents perfectly. Cook in the oven at 200°C (400°F) mark 6 for 10 - 15 minutes depending on the size of the mushrooms.

Serve the mushrooms wrapped in the foil.

Mediterranean sun produces an abundance of fresh figs

RISOTTO WITH GREEN PEPPER, WALNUTS AND VIN SANTO
Risotto ai Peperoni con Noci e Vin Santo

The people from Siena were the first to cook with spices in Italy. This new recipe from Spaltenna has a very fine ingredient: green pepper in its own liquid. Ideally, pick fresh walnuts when they are still green in their shell. After cracking the shell, peel the skin away from the nut and mince, not too finely, keep a few whole ones for garnish. If fresh walnuts are not available, dry ones can be used. They will add a spicier flavour to the risotto.

50g (2 oz) butter
1 medium-sized onion, thinly sliced
5ml (1 tsp) green pepper, pressed in a pestle and mortar
40g (1$^{1}/_{2}$ oz) shelled walnuts, coarsely minced
350g (12 oz) camaroli or risotto rice
125ml (4 fl oz) Vin Santo
1 litre (1$^{3}/_{4}$ pints) vegetable stock
grated Parmesan cheese
extra butter, to serve

SERVES 4 - 6

Melt the butter with 3 - 4 teaspoons of water and sauté the onion until it is translucent. Add the green pepper and walnuts, and simmer for 1 - 2 minutes.

Add the rice and simmer until it becomes golden. Then pour about three-quarters of the Vin Santo over the rice and leave to reduce. Stir in the stock and simmer until the rice is almost cooked. Then add the remaining Vin Santo and cook until the rice is *al dente*.

Turn off the heat and stir in plenty of Parmesan cheese and butter. Let the mixture cool for 2 - 3 minutes so that the rice absorbs the juices before serving.

CHEESE AND WALNUT SALAD
Insalata con Pecorino e Noci

400g (14 oz) mature Pecorino cheese
2 fennel bulbs
12 whole walnuts
about 45ml (3 tbsp) extra virgin olive oil
rocket and other small green salad leaves

SERVES 4

Cut the cheese and fennel bulbs into very thin slices. Arrange the salad leaves around the edge of a serving dish. Put the slices of cheese and fennel in the centre and the walnuts on top. Sprinkle the oil over the salad and serve.

COUNTRY SALAD WITH TUSCAN PROSCIUTTO
Insalata di Campo con Prosciutto Toscano

1/2 head crisp lettuce
75g (3 oz) radicchio
75g (3 oz) wild or mixed baby salad leaves
50g (2 oz) rocket
45ml (3 tbsp) extra virgin olive oil
salt and freshly ground black pepper
20g (3/4 oz) butter
100g (4 oz) Tuscan prosciutto, diced small
20ml (4 tsp) red wine vinegar

SERVES 4

Rinse the salad leaves thoroughly, drain and dry carefully. Cut into thin slices and put in a mixing bowl. Stir the oil, salt and pepper with a fork and add to the salad leaves, tossing until they are well coated. Divide into portions.

Melt the butter in a frying pan and simmer the prosciutto over a low heat for a few minutes, then add the vinegar and cook for a few seconds more. Divide the vinegar- flavoured prosciutto between the portions of salad.

From Monsanto to Florence

Our farewell to Spaltenna was an exuberant evening barbecue on a wild and tempestuous night. The wind whipped the charcoal grill into a frenzy; there was a jam session, complete with Seamus on the bongos, and a respectable amount of Guinness was drunk, mostly by the Italian guests. Then we headed west, straight across Chianti towards the big, unpretty market town of Poggibonsi to our next destination, Monsanto.

Like Spaltenna, there is a spectacular Romanesque church in Monsanto – San Ruffiniano a Monsanto, one of the oldest churches in Chianti – and a beautiful castle, the Castello di Monsanto. Monsanto is what I would call a decorative, residential castle with splendid terraced gardens and sweeping views across the vine-covered hills. The property belongs to a prosperous family of northern Italian textile manufactures, the Bianchis. Fabrizio Bianchi began redeveloping the estate with his father in the early sixties, reconstructing farm buildings, working on new wine cellars, and planting and replanting vineyards and olive groves. Today the estate wines are particularly highly rated by American wine buyers. The most famous Monsanto product is a Chianti Classico Riserva called 'Il Poggio' made from a blend of Sangiovese, Canaiolo and Colorino grapes, which grow beautifully in the heavy clay soil. They also produce a range of altogether more newfangled wines like Nemo, a cabernet sauvignon that matures in small oak casks.

Lauara Bianchi, Fabrizio's twenty-something-ish law-graduate daughter, looks after the day-to-day running of the estate, and her mother Giuliana, along with the family cook Rosana, turns out masterful Tuscan food. The obvious irony is that you sit at lunch with a rich and accomplished family in a magnificent house eating what would

A seductive meal - pappa al pomodoro followed by spit-roasted chicken

be peasant food anywhere else, but of course this is Tuscany. We began with a fabulously good pappa al pomodoro, a seductive mush concocted from olive oil, garlic, fresh tomatoes and stale bread, liberally flavoured with olive oil and fresh basil. Afterwards there was succulent and crispy roasted chicken, cooked on a spit over a wood fire. This is Tuscan food at its best: unadorned, unfussy, irreproachable.

If you like a lot of pretence and palaver, this cooking isn't for you. Whereas a lot of cookery tends to be about social status and display, Tuscan cooking is really only about flavour: that's why you get grand people eating like peasants, or perhaps it might be more accurate to say that you get peasants eating like grand people. Food in Italy tends not to be socially divisive.

Giuliana also showed us another elemental soup, zuppa

de farro, a rich concoction made from spelt, one of the more ancient and less well known members of the wheat family. As with pappa al pomodoro there is little technique and few ingredients: farro, beans, water, garlic, celery, onions, carrot, a bit of tomato paste, a few sage leaves and a final shot of olive oil. It was time to go and we began the short journey north to Florence.

It is hard to describe this captivating, handsome, infuriating and compelling city. It might be tempting to begin by saying that centuries of being one of the top tourist attractions in the world have given Florence the status of a film star and the manners of a whore, but that wouldn't take account of the city's often well-hidden pleasures. Let's say that Florence can be a difficult city: a place that people approach full of hope and high expectations and sometimes leave with relief.

Aldous Huxley, author of *Brave New World*, was distinctly underwhelmed by Florence. 'We came back through Florence,' he wrote, 'and the spectacle of that second rate provincial town with its repulsive Gothic architecture and its acres of Christmas card primitives made me almost sick. The only points about Florence are the country outside it, the Michelangelo tombs, Brunelleschi's dome and a few rare pictures. The rest is simply dung when compared to Rome.'

I'm not sure why Huxley had such a miserable time in the city of flowers, but even the keenest and most good-humoured visitor can crack under the burden of scowls, queues, high prices, and often rather poor facilities on offer. Then there is the danger of Stendhal's syndrome – so called because the 19th-century French novelist Stendhal was the first to describe it – in which the sheer amount of culture to be absorbed, and beauty to be appreciated, causes a disabling mental panic.

On the plus side, the city that invented the Renaissance has enough beautiful and moving works of art to keep anyone entranced for a lifetime. There are marvellous things to buy: from the fashionable fripperies of the Via de Tornabuoni (the Bond Street of Florence) to the unequalled picture frames carved by Signor Moscardi and his rivals, to the precious soaps and shampoos on offer at the historic Antica Farmacia di Santa Maria Novella. Florence is a city of culture, but it has long been a city of commerce too. It was one of the earliest centres for banking, and traditional crafts of leatherwork, woodcarving and silver-smithing still flourish. The whole place has been described as the world's largest outdoor museum, but it is also a bustling modern city, with all the problems of bustling modern Italian cities.

You can eat well in Florence, and good grief, you can eat appallingly. Don't go to Florence expecting a sophisticated cuisine. What you will get here is essentially the same sort of plain, rustic country cooking that we ate in Chianti. The real food of Florence is simple, severe and delicious – take the most famous dish of all, bistecca alla Fiorentina, a dish that is frequently discussed and argued about without cease. What is it? A T-bone steak, grilled and put on a plate. Our first stop on the steak trail was Il Latini, an unadorned neighbourhood restaurant celebrated as a gathering place for literary, Bohemian Florence. Whilst the patriarchal Narciso Latini minded the espresso machine at the bar, his son Giovanni demonstrated the essence of a good bistecca alla Fiorentina. The word, bistecca, by the way, is an Italian tribute to the English beefsteak. You begin with a side of beef from Chianina cattle, the native Tuscan favourite. 'The beef must be hung for exactly 15 days in a fridge with a temperature of between two and three degrees centigrade,' Giovanni says, 'then the steak has to be cut by hand with an old fashioned butcher's knife just before cooking.' An electric saw is no good, he explains, because the high speed of the blade heats the meat as it is being cut and ruins the flavour. Having cut your T-bone – and these steaks are huge, about one and a half inches thick, weighing about a kilogram each – the next step is to cook it.

So off we went to the generally acclaimed shrine of the bistecca, the Buca di Lapi, a steak joint successful enough to have a sister restaurant in Philadelphia. Down a steep flight of stairs – 'Buca' means a hole in the ground – we found a team of chefs working at the big charcoal grill. The secret of cooking a bistecca Fiorentina is really to do as little as possible. The steak is put on to a very hot grill, cooked for about five minutes and then turned over. The cooked side is sprinkled with salt. After another three or four minutes, the steak comes off the grill. The last side to be cooked is salted, and it is finished. Some cooks rub the steak with peppercorns or garlic cloves, some drizzle olive oil on it either before or after, but my own experience prefers the simple equation that the best beef with the least flavouring makes the most authentic bistecca Fiorentina. It is most important not to disturb the steak while it cooks, because any poking, prodding or handling causes the beef to lose the juices that give it much of its flavour. You can't really cook this sort of steak on the feeble heat of a domestic grill: wait until the warm weather and barbecue.

Eating in Florence will quickly disabuse you of many the clichés of Italian cooking. There is very little pasta on menus and the odd risotto is a relatively recent northern intruder. You will eat a lot of soup, a lot of beans and a lot of protein. You will also frequently begin your meals with crostini, the distinctive Tuscan canapes that along with their close relation, bruschetta, have become immensely fashionable all over the world in the last four or five years.

Bruschetta is really a Roman speciality. Toast a thick slice of bread, rub it with a clove of garlic, pour on the best olive oil you can find, and that's bruschetta. You can tart it up with some chopped ripe plum tomatoes sprinkled with some freshly torn basil. Crostini begin with toast as well, although the bread should be thinner. You then spread your toast with chicken liver pâté, truffle butter or any savoury concoction that appeals to you. You can use thicker bread to make crostini, which can be topped with lentils (as we ate in Norcia), or with white beans cooked with a little sage.

You will eat crostini and other simple, but rather refined food, at the little Cantinetta Antinori in Florence, an extremely elegant wine bar owned by the famous wine-

Warmth, wine and crostini topped with lentils

making Antinori family. It is my favourite, and the most delicious watering hole in this sometimes hostile city. Like our peasant's lunch amidst the glamour of Castello di Monsanto, the simple country food of the Cantinetta Antinori fits right into a sophisticated ambience, because that is the Tuscan way of eating.

Even those who find the food in Florence rather uninspiring are left speechless after a snack at Vivoli. After a lifetime's research, I am convinced they are simply the best ice-cream makers in the world. The ice cream shop itself is flashy and uncomfortably crowded; the best thing to do is buy your coppa or cornetto and sit on the steps of the conveniently under-used church just across the road. My own nomination for their greatest flavour is fig, but you will have your own ideas.

BEEF STEW WITH POTATOES
Spezzatino con Patate

For the stew
40g (1¹/₂ oz) dried ceps
45ml (3 tbsp) extra virgin olive oil
2 onions finely chopped
2-3 sprigs fresh sage and rosemary, chopped
600g (1¹/₄ lb) stewing beef, cut into cubes
250ml (8 fl oz) red wine
5ml (1 tsp) tomato purée
200g (7 oz) plum tomatoes, peeled and chopped
15ml (1 tbsp) chopped fresh basil
350ml (12 fl oz) vegetable stock
salt and freshly ground black pepper

For the potatoes
40g (1¹/₂ oz) pork lard
4 cloves garlic, chopped
1-2 sprigs rosemary and sage, chopped
5ml (1 tsp) tomato purée
100g (4 oz) plum tomatoes
500g (18 oz) potatoes, peeled and quartered
about 450ml (³/₄ pint) vegetable stock

SERVES 4

Soak the ceps in warm water for 20 minutes and rinse thoroughly in running water. Drain. Heat the oil in a large saucepan and sauté the onions and herbs. Add the beef and cook until golden. Then add the ceps, wine and tomato purée and stir well. Allow the mixture to thicken over a moderate heat. After about 5 minutes, add the tomatoes, basil, and stock, and seasoning. Cook over a low heat for about 2 hours.

Melt the lard and sauté the garlic and herbs. Stir in the tomato purée and tomatoes. Then add the potatoes and cover with stock. Season and simmer for about 20 minutes until the potatoes are tender. Serve with the beef stew.

GARLIC BREAD WITH FRESH TOMATO
Pomodoro Fresco Fettunta

450g (1 lb) fresh tomatoes
75ml (5 tbsp) olive oil
30ml (2 tbsp) chopped fresh oregano
30ml (2 tbsp)chopped fresh basil
salt and freshly ground black pepper
3 cloves garlic, peeled
8 thick slices white bread

SERVES 4

Pour boiling water over the tomatoes, leave for a minute and then remove the skins and seeds. Chop the tomatoes into small pieces and add some olive oil, oregano, basil, salt, pepper and some whole cloves of garlic. Chill in the refrigerator for 2 hours until the tomatoes have absorbed the flavours.

Meanwhile, toast the white bread slices on both sides. Rub the remaining garlic over the bread, drizzle over the remaining olive oil and sprinkle with salt. Serve topped with the chilled tomato mixture.

CHICKEN ROASTED IN CHIANTI
Galletto al Chianti

1 roasting chicken, about 1.4 kg (3 lb)
45ml (3 tbsp) olive oil
4 or 5 cloves garlic
salt and freshly ground black pepper
1 bottle Chianti Classico wine
fresh rosemary and sage
125 ml (4 fl oz) red wine vinegar
30 ml (2 tbsp) plain flour

SERVES 4

Wash the chicken, pat it dry with paper towels and divide it into eight pieces. Heat the oil in a large saucepan and sauté the garlic and herbs in olive oil. Add the chicken pieces, season with salt and pepper, and cook until golden. Remove the chicken pieces from the pan and transfer to a flameproof casserole.

Pour in sufficient Chianti to cover the chicken, add the red wine vinegar and season with the herbs, and more salt and pepper if necessary. Simmer gently for about 30 minutes.

Remove the chicken from the casserole and keep warm.

Blend the flour with a little water to a smoothe paste, then stir into the cooking liquid in the casserole. Cook for about 5 minutes stirring occasionally. Pass the liquid through a fine sieve, and reheat with the chicken for 5-10 minutes. Serve hot.

FLORENTINE TRIPE
Trippa alla Fiorentina

250ml (8 fl oz) extra virgin olive oil
2 onions, finely chopped
5ml (1 tsp) tomato paste
500g (18 oz) plum tomatoes, peeled and chopped
salt and freshly ground black pepper
700g (1³/₄ lb) cooked tripe, sliced
50g (2 oz) butter
100g (4oz) Parmesan cheese, freshly grated
300ml (¹/₂ pint) vegetable stock

SERVES 4

Heat the oil in a large saucepan and sauté the onion until softened. Then add the tomato paste and tomatoes, and season with salt and pepper. Stir in the tripe, butter and stock. Allow to boil for several minutes, and serve hot with grated Parmesan cheese on top.

FLORENTINE POT ROAST
Stracotto alla Fiorentina

600g (1¹/₄ lb) topside of beef
1 stick celery, finely chopped
4 carrots, finely chopped
50g (2 oz) bacon, finely chopped
500ml (18 fl oz) olive oil
3 cloves garlic
2 onions, finely chopped
2-3 sprigs fresh sage and rosemary, chopped
2 litres (3¹/₂ pints) Chianti wine
1kg (2¹/₄ lb) canned plum tomatoes
6 basil leaves

SERVES 4

Make small incisions in the side of the meat, insert half the celery, the carrots and bacon in the holes. Tie the meat up compactly for roasting.

Heat the oil in a flameproof casserole and sauté the onions, garlic, the remaining celery and the sage and rosemary until softened. Add the meat and cook for about 15 minutes. Pour in the wine slowly and continue to cook, turning the meat frequently so that it does not stick, until the sauce has thickened. Then add the tomatoes and basil, and cook for a few minutes. Cover the casserole and cook over a low heat for about 2 hours. Check frequently that the meat is covered with the tomato sauce, and has not stuck to the casserole.

Remove the meat from the casserole and pass the sauce through a fine sieve. Cut the meat in slices and pour the sauce over. Serve hot.

FLORENTINE PANCAKES
Crespelle alla Fiorentina

For the pancakes
100g (4 oz) plain flour
225ml (10 fl oz) milk
salt
1 egg and an egg yolk
50g (2 oz) unsalted butter, melted

For the filling
500g (18 oz) fresh Ricotta cheese
500g (18 oz) fresh spinach, chopped
6 eggs, beaten
150g (5 oz) Parmesan cheese, freshly grated
100g (4 oz) plain flour

For the white sauce
75g (3 oz) butter
90g (3½ oz) plain flour
1 litre (1¾ pints) milk
ground nutmeg

For finishing
fresh tomato sauce
grated Parmesan cheese and melted butter

SERVES 4

Mix the flour, milk, egg, a little melted butter, and salt together to make the batter. Using the remaining melted butter to grease a heavy frying pan, make thin pancakes. Blend the ingredients together for the filling. Using a spatula, spread some of the filling on each pancake and roll. Cut into slices. To make the white sauce, melt the butter in a saucepan, add the flour and make a roux. Add the milk gradually, beating well, and season with nutmeg and salt. Layer the white sauce and pancakes in an ovenproof dish, finishing with a layer of white sauce. Top with a little tomato sauce, grated Parmesan cheese and melted butter. Cook in the oven at 220°C (425°F) mark 7 for about 15-20 minutes.

TOMATO BREAD SOUP

Minestra di Pomodori con Pane

100ml (4 fl oz) extra virgin olive oil
4 cloves garlic, finely chopped
1 leek, finely chopped
1 red chilli pepper, finely chopped
1kg (2¼ lb) can peeled plum tomatoes
15ml (1 tbsp) tomato purée
600ml (1 pint) vegetable stock
salt and freshly ground black pepper
50g (2 oz) fresh basil
500g (18 oz) white Tuscan bread
(unsalted), sliced

SERVES 4

Heat the oil in a large saucepan and sauté the garlic, leek and red chilli pepper. Add the tomatoes and tomato purée and cook over a high heat for about 10 minutes, stirring constantly.

Add the vegetable stock, season with salt and pepper, bring to the boil, and boil for 5 minutes. Add the basil.

Remove from the heat and add the slices of bread, blending well with the tomatoes, and then leave to stand for about 30 minutes. Whisk thoroughly until perfectly blended.

Serve either reheated or at room temperature, adding a few drops of extra virgin olive oil to each portion at the moment of serving.

TUSCAN BREAD AND TOMATO SALAD
Panzanella

½ loaf day-old bread
60ml (4 tbsp) red wine vinegar
8 ripe red tomatoes, chopped
1 small red onion, chopped
head of iceberg lettuce or cos lettuce, chopped
25g (1 oz) fresh basil leaves, torn
extra virgin olive oil
salt and freshly ground black pepper

SERVES 4

Break the dry bread into chunks and soak for 2-3 hours in water to which the vinegar has been added. Then wring out the liquid with your hands and crumble the bread into a large salad bowl. Add the tomatoes, onion, lettuce and basil. Dress with oil, salt and pepper. Keep chilled before serving.

FRIED COURGETTES AND COURGETTE FLOWERS
Pastella con Zucchini e Fiori Fritti

60ml (4 tbsp) unbleached, plain flour
60ml (4 tbsp) water
pinch of salt
6 small courgettes, cut into strips or sliced
6 courgette flowers
olive oil for frying

SERVES 6

Make a fairly loose batter with the flour, water and salt, mixing thoroughly. Heat some oil in a deep-fat fryer to 195°C (385°F). Dip the strips or slices of courgette and the flowers in the batter before frying them in the olive oil. Be careful not to crowd them in the pan. Remove them from the pan as soon as they start to brown. Drain on paper towels and serve immediately.

BITTER CHOCOLATE ICE CREAM
Gelato di Cioccolatta Amara

8 egg yolks
175g/6 oz caster sugar
1 litre (1³/₄ pints) milk
200g (7 oz) bitter chocolate, broken into small pieces
250g (9 oz) cocoa powder
50g (2 oz) caramelised sugar

SERVES 4-6

Beat the egg yolks and sugar together until very thick. Pour the milk into a saucepan, add the chocolate and cocoa and bring to the boil slowly, stirring constantly to ensure a perfectly blended mixture. Remove from the heat and beat in the egg yolk mixture while the chocolate-flavoured milk is still hot. Pour the mixture into a freezer container. Freeze for 2-3 hours until beginning to firm up, then whisk thoroughly. Add the caramelised sugar and freeze until solid.

CHOCOLATE SAUCE
Salsa di Cioccolatta

300g (11 oz) plain chocolate
250ml (8 fl oz) milk

Melt the chocolate in the top of a double saucepan over a low heat. Add the milk and mix thoroughly. Cook for a few minutes and then set aside, stirring occasionally until cool. Serve at room temperature.

'PRIEST-STRANGLERS' IN WILD MUSHROOM SAUCE

Strozzapreti in Salsa di Funghi Finferli o Chiodini

For the pasta
350g (12 oz) unbleached white flour
125ml (4 fl oz) water
125ml (4 fl oz) milk
pinch of salt

For the sauce
25-40g (1-1½ oz) butter
450g (1 lb) wild mushrooms, cleaned and chopped
1 clove garlic, minced
45ml (3 tbsp) single cream
15ml (1 tbsp) chopped parsley

SERVES 6

To make the pasta, mound the flour on a wooden board and form a well in the centre. Mix the water and milk together and pour into the centre of the well. Supporting the sides of the well with your left hand, use a fork to incorporate the flour from the sides of the well into the milk-and-water mixture. Stir in more and more of the flour until it forms a loose dough; then begin to knead the dough with the heel of your hand, gathering the flour and scraps of dough into a ball. Knead for a few minutes until it is well amalgamated. Continue kneading until the dough is smooth and elastic, and then roll the pasta out with a long rolling pin. It should be as thin as possible and virtually transparent.

Alternatively, you may use a pasta machine to finish the kneading and rolling of the pasta. First, with the rollers at the widest setting, halve the ball of dough and pass each half through the rollers eight or nine times, folding the length of dough into thirds each time, dusting it with flour and re-passing it through the rollers. When the dough is smooth and elastic, begin to roll out the dough by passing it successively through each of the settings, lightly flouring between passes, until the finest setting is reached. Cut the ribbon of dough in half and pass for the final time through the finest setting. Carefully lay the dough over the back of a chair and cover with a clean tea-towel.

Then, working with one piece of dough at a time, cut the pasta into strips about 2-2.5cm ($^3/_4$-1 inch) wide by 7.5-10cm (3-4 inches) long. With the palm of your hand, roll the strips of dough diagonally to give them a slight twist. Set aside on a clean tea-towel. Continue with the next piece of dough.

If you don't have the time or patience to make fresh pasta, substitute good-quality dried pasta spirals.

Bring a large pan of water to the boil. Cook the pasta briefly until *al dente*. Drain well and divide into 6 servings. Top with the mushroom sauce and hand Parmesan cheese separately.

To make the mushroom sauce, melt the butter in a wide frying pan and add the mushrooms and garlic. Cook for 10 minutes. Then stir in the cream and parsley, and cook for a further 5 minutes.

COOKED CREAM WITH STRAWBERRY SAUCE
Panna Cotta con Salsa di Fragole

3 sheets gelatine
475ml (16 fl oz) double cream
250ml (8 fl oz) milk
45ml (3 tbsp) caster sugar
For the sauce
300g (11 oz) strawberries
30ml (2 tbsp) caster sugar
30ml (2 tbsp) brandy

SERVES 6

Soften the gelatine in cold water for about 10 minutes.

Heat the cream and milk with the sugar in a saucepan until the mixture reaches boiling point. Immediately remove from the heat. Squeeze the water out of the gelatine sheets and stir the gelatine into the hot cream mixture, whisking until the gelatine is completely dissolved.

Pour the cream mixture into individual 125ml (4 fl oz) moulds and chill in the refrigerator for at least 3 hours before serving.

To make the sauce, purée the strawberries in a food processor. Add the sugar and taste for sweetness. Transfer to a saucepan and cook over a moderate heat for 10 minutes. Remove from heat and stir in the brandy.

To serve, unmould the *panna cotta* on to dessert plates and spoon the sauce around each cream.

CHESTNUT FLOUR CAKE
Castagnaccio

45ml (3 tbsp) raisins
125ml (4 fl oz) lukewarm milk
250g (9 oz) chestnut flour
15ml (1 tbsp) granulated sugar
pinch of salt
30ml (2 tbsp) pine nuts and/or walnuts
250ml (8 fl oz) cold milk
45ml (3 tbsp) olive oil
15ml (1 tbsp) rosemary leaves

SERVES 6

Soak the raisins in the lukewarm milk for 20 minutes.
Reserve 15ml (1 tbsp) of the chestnut flour and sift the rest into a large mixing bowl. Add the sugar, salt and nuts. Mix well with a wooden spoon, adding the cold milk slowly as you stir.

Drain the raisins and coat with the remaining chestnut flour. Add to the mixture in the bowl with 30ml (2 tbsp) of the olive oil and mix well to a smooth, thin batter.

Brush a 25cm (10 inch) shallow round cake tin with olive oil and preheat the oven to 200°C (400°F) mark 6.

Pour the cake mixture into the tin, drizzle with the remaining olive oil and sprinkle with rosemary leaves. Bake for 40-50 minutes, or until the surface cracks slightly. Remove from the oven and allow to rest for about 20 minutes before serving it directly from the tin, cut in slices like a pie.

RISOTTO CANTINETTA-STYLE
Risotto alla Cantinetta

30ml (2 tbsp) extra virgin olive oil
1 onion, finely chopped
300g (11 oz) risotto rice
125ml (4 fl oz) dry white wine
750ml (1¼ pint) beef stock
2 Italian sausages, sliced
100g (4 oz) cooked ham, diced
50g (2 oz) butter
1 head red radicchio, cut into julienne
15ml (1 tbsp) chopped fresh basil
freshly grated Parmesan cheese

SERVES 4

Heat the oil in a frying pan and sauté the onion until soft. Add the rice and cook gently until golden, stirring constantly. Pour in the wine and allow to cook briefly. Ladle in the beef stock, stirring after each addition, allowing each ladleful to absorb, before adding the next, and simmer for about 20 minutes in all.

Meanwhile, sauté the sausages and ham in the butter before adding to the rice mixture.

When the rice is almost cooked (keep tasting to check) and is *al dente*, add the julienne strips of radicchio and the basil.

Serve with freshly grated Parmesan cheese.

VEGETABLE BREAD SOUP
Ribollita

150ml (¹/₄ pint) extra virgin olive oil
1 onion, finely chopped
3-4 sprigs summer savory
1 thick slice of ham skin
30ml (2 tbsp) tomato purée
200g (7 oz) tomatoes, peeled
2 carrots, chopped
2 potatoes, chopped
¹/₂ stick celery, chopped
¹/₂ white cabbage, shredded
175g (6 oz) Swiss chard (or spinach), shredded
75g (3 oz) kale, shredded
500g (18 oz) puréed cannellini beans
200g (7 oz) whole cannellini beans
1 litre (2 pints) vegetable stock
salt and freshly ground black pepper
¹/₂ loaf day-old Tuscan bread (unsalted)
60ml (4 tbsp) fresh chopped basil

SERVES 4 - 6

Heat half of the olive oil in a large saucepan and sauté the onion with the summer savory and ham skin. Add the tomato purée, peeled tomatoes and cook for several minutes. Stir in the carrots, potatoes and celery. Add the remaining vegetables, for a few minutes, and then add the beans and sufficient stock to cover the vegetables. Bring to the boil and then simmer for about 2 hours. Season with salt and pepper.

Layer the bread slices in a large bowl with the vegetable mixture, softening each layer with a little of the olive oil. Return the bread and vegetable mixture to the saucepan and cook gently for a further 10 minutes. Leave to stand, covered, until ready to serve, having stirred the mixture carefully to ensure the bread slices are well coated.

Serve directly from the saucepan into bowls, adding a last touch of olive oil and a scattering of basil to each portion.

PASTA AND CHICK-PEA SOUP
Pasta e Ceci

400g (14 oz) chick-peas
30ml (2 tbsp) olive oil
2 onions, chopped
2 sprigs fresh rosemary
about 600ml (1 pint) meat stock
salt and freshly ground black pepper
100g (4 oz) very small soup pasta *ditaloni rigati*

SERVES 4

Soak the chick-peas overnight in cold water, drain and put into a saucepan. Cover with fresh water and boil until tender, about 1¹/₂ hours. Heat the olive oil in a large saucepan and sauté the onions and rosemary. Purée three-quarters of the chick-peas in a food processor or blender, leaving the remaining quarter whole. Put all the chick-peas into the saucepan with the onion. Thin the soup to the required consistency with the stock, season with salt and pepper and simmer gently for about 30 minutes. Add the soup pasta and simmer until it is cooked. Serve with a little olive oil added to each portion.

VEAL FRICASSEE
Bocconcini di Vitello in Fricassea

45ml (3 tbsp) olive oil
1 medium-sized onion, finely chopped
600g (1¹/₄ lb) veal shoulder, cut into cubes
125ml (4 fl oz) dry white wine
500ml (18 fl oz) milk
50g (2 oz) plain flour
juice of 1 lemon
2 egg yolks
250ml (8 fl oz) double cream
salt and freshly ground black pepper

SERVES 4

Heat the oil in a large saucepan and sauté the onion until golden brown. Then add the veal. Cook over a moderate heat for about 15 minutes. Pour in the wine and cook until evaporated. Mix the milk and flour into a thin paste, and blend with the meat mixture. Simmer for about 1 hour.

Mix the lemon juice, egg yolks and cream together and add to the meat.

Season to taste and serve hot with boiled potatoes.

DEEP-FRIED 'RAGS'
Cenci

350g (12 oz) unbleached plain flour
2 large eggs, beaten
45ml (3 tbsp) olive oil
30ml (2 tbsp) white rum
pinch of salt
100g (4 oz) caster sugar
1 litre ($1^3/_4$ pints) vegetable oil
75g (3 oz) icing sugar, sifted

SERVES 6

Mound the flour on a large wooden board and make a well in the centre. Put the eggs, oil, rum, salt and sugar into the well and mix all the ingredients with a fork, slowly working outwards until all are blended. Knead the dough for about 20 minutes until very smooth and leave to rest, covered with a clean tea-towel, for about 1 hour.

Roll out the dough, about 5cm (2 inches) thick, and cut into two finger-width rectangles using a pastry wheel.

Heat the vegetable oil to 180°C (350°F) in a deep fryer and fry the rectangles, one at a time. When golden-coloured (about 1 minute), remove and place on paper towels to drain.

Sprinkle the rectangles with icing sugar and serve.

To Bologna

Travelling north from Florence you leave Tuscany and enter a different Italy – the autostrada threads through a wide band of the Apennine mountains and descends into the broad plains of Emilia-Romagna. This is the region – really two regions, Emilia in the west and Romagna along the coast – that is home to Parma ham, Parmesan cheese, tagliatelle, tortellini, balsamic vinegar; all are among the most famous dishes and ingredients in the Italian culinary repertoire. Italians rarely agree about anything gastronomic, but many are grudgingly willing to admit that the best food in Italy is found here. Geography makes this one of the lushest farming areas in the country, and the largely flat terrain of the Po valley makes agriculture a bit less arduous than in the rest of this largely mountainous country. This is a land of fat; one of the few parts of Italy where butter and olive oil, and even lard, co-exist in rich abundance.

To start, we need a little history. The Roman politician and soldier, Marcus Aemilius Lepidus, built a heroic road, 250 kilometres straight as a gun barrel from Ariminum (the Roman name for Rimini) on the Adriatic coast to Palacentia (the modern day Piacenza) just south of Milan. The major towns and cities of Emilia-Romagna are strung out along this road with Roman military precision at roughly 40 kilometre intervals. In the middle of them all and dominating the whole region is Bologna, an inexplicably under-visited city of extreme architectural, artistic, historical and culinary fascination. And a jolly good place to go shopping as well.

Bologna is full of nicknames. It is celebrated as Bologna 'the Learned' because it is the home of Europe's oldest university. Legendarily founded in 425 AD, the university is well known for law and medicine; its roster of illustrious past students includes the great poet Petrach and the astronomer Copernicus. One of its 12th-century graduates founded the law school at Oxford. So Bologna's donnish reputation is well founded.

The city's artistic reputation will never stand as high as that of Rome or Florence or Venice, but the National Art Gallery of Bologna is home to a number of great paintings, unsurprisingly dominated by the artists of the Bolognese school: painters like Guido Reni and the talented Carracci brothers.

Architecturally the city has a lot to offer, with medieval towers of dizzying heights and a fantastically extensive 20-mile network of arcaded streets so you can stroll and shop in comfort in what must be Italy's rainiest city.

Bologna is also celebrated as Bologna 'the Red', a nickname which reflects leftwing domination of the city's politics from the fall of fascism up to the present. Finally it is Bologna 'the Fat' because this is a city where even by Italian standards, food is an obsession. They say that what a Roman eats in a week, a Bolognese eats in a day. I believe it.

Let's dispel a myth – the myth of spaghetti Bolognese. Everyone in Britain has eaten spaghetti Bolognese, but no one in Bologna has. If you ask for spaghetti Bolognese here, you are looked at with horror and incomprehension. 'Spaghetti Bolognese?' they say, 'but there is no such thing. In Bologna you eat tagliatelle Bolognese'! And indeed you do. We're now in the land of fresh pasta. Unlike the dried pasta of the south which is made from hard wheat and water, the fresh pasta of Emilia-Romagna is made with eggs and the soft wheat which grows so abundantly here.

Tagliatelle, long flat noodles about a quarter of an inch wide, are the favourite local pasta shape. In Bologna they're habitually served with a rich meaty ragu which we know as a Bolognese sauce. Like all the other iconic dishes of the Italian cooking there is a howling debate about what makes a real Bolognese sauce. It is certainly not merely a bit of fried mince with tomato sauce. Indeed a ragu is emphatically not a tomato sauce at all; it is a meat sauce. The most traditional recipes tend to begin with a base of

The Biagis, each wearing the 'Tortellino d'Oro'

celery, carrot, onion and prosciutto cooked in a little butter. Minced veal, tomatoes and nutmeg go in next and then a bit of cream.

Other equally traditional recipes call for the meat to be simmered in milk and to add pancetta (a part of pig belly rather like bacon), white wine or lemon zest, to the list of ingredients. Most cooks agree that the sauce ought to be cooked in an earthenware crock and that long, slow cooking – at the very least two or three hours at a gentle simmer – is absolutely vital. The result is a rich, powerfully-flavoured sauce that contrasts vividly with the eggy delicacy of top class home-made tagliatelle.

When you get your plateful of tagliatelle, which in Bologna is guaranteed to be formidable, you generously

Hand-made tortellini for sale

sprinkle it with freshly grated Parmesan cheese and dig in.
I have seen Bolognese eat their tagliatelle with astonishing
speed before progressing on to their main course, but I
find that even after the most refined tagliatelle with ragu
alla Bolognese, I could use a little nap or certainly no
more than a green salad.

There are lighter, more 'modern' versions of ragu alla
bolognese, but once they start to lose the richness and pro-
fundity of the original, there's hardly any point in eating
them. At this stage you may be tempted to say 'so what? It's
only a sauce, it's not the secret of eternal youth'. Well one
of the things Italian cooking has to teach us is that everything, every element of a dish, is important. The German
architect Mies van der Rohe had a saying that 'God is in

the details'. You could apply this saying to the cookery of any part of Italy. Cookery has to be performed with love and passion otherwise it's better not performed at all.

The other great pasta dish of Bologna is tortellini, little stuffed pasta which can reach astonishing heights of delicacy and sophistication. The best place to eat these wonders is the Ristorante Biagi just on the outskirts of Bologna, on the way to the south-bound autostrada. It looks like a cross between a truck stop and a motorway service station. There's a small counter at the front window dispensing ice cream and there's also a standard issue Italian bar with espresso machine, little plates of sticky pastries and rows of obscure aperitifs and digestifs lining the shelves. Behind the bar is a little dining room. The place looks undistinguished but you get hungry as soon as you walk through the door. If you scan the walls keenly you will find a jewel-like tortellino elaborately framed. This is the 'Tortellino d'Oro', the golden tortellino, the Oscar or maybe even the Nobel Prize of the pasta world.

No one is really sure about the antiquity of tortellini. Legend has it that they were invented in ancient times. Venus, the goddess of beauty, stopped for the night at an inn near Bologna. As she slept, the innkeeper peeped through the keyhole of her bedroom and saw the goddess's naked body sprawled across the bed. He went to his kitchen and prepared a pasta modelled on her beautiful navel, and this was the first tortellino. There are other apocryphal tales about the birth of tortellini but they all agree that it is a tribute to the navel of a beautiful woman.

In the kitchen of the Ristorante Biagi, a team of women make tiny tortellini, shaping them around their finger tips. The Biagi tortellini are so finely made and so Lilliputian that a tablespoon will hold 18 of them. Tortellini pay tribute to Bologna's rich tradition of pig butchery (as does the industrially produced American luncheon meat, baloney, a corruption of the word Bologna). The little pastas are filled with prosciutto, mortadella (a large, fatty pork sausage), beef and cheese. Sometimes pork, turkey or chicken find their way into the filling as well. Tortellini may be served with sauce, but they are most properly, beautifully and simply presented 'in brodo' surrounded by a pale golden stock which can either be based on chicken or beef. The obligatory sprinkling of Parmesan follows. I must confess to eating two platefuls of the stuff when I visited Biagi. I must also confess that during a brief stint in the kitchen, I failed miserably to mould even one acceptable tortellino whilst all around me they were being made with speed, grace and exactitude. Biagi, it must be said, also makes some of the best ice cream in Italy; perhaps slightly less ambrosial than Vivoli in Florence, but only by a hair. Their sweet cream ice cream is a real marvel.

I must explain a little bit about prosciutto, which figures in so many Bolognese recipes. It is most commonly called Parma ham, but it is hardly mere ham. Like many other basic ingredients in Italy, prosciutto is produced with a fanatical attention to detail and quality. Real prosciutto di Parma is produced in a strictly defined area just to the north-west of Bologna. Although the city of Parma is a lot smaller than Bologna, it is also refreshingly undiscovered and has much to offer in the way of culture and gastronomy. As you would expect from the birthplace of Toscanini, there is an excellent opera house, the Teatro Regio, built in the early 19th century.

The fat, healthy pigs that live in the countryside around Parma are the raw material for this superlative ham. The pigs are fed mostly on the whey that's left over from the making of Parmesan cheese, the other emblematic local product which we will discuss in the next chapter. The most important characteristic of a Parma ham is the extremely tricky balance between salt and sweet flavours. More salt means a longer lasting ham, but a coarser flavour. Unlike many mass produced hams, this doesn't have any sugar or nitrates used in its cure. Parma hams are made by just the right formula which results in a powerful, but almost nutty flavour. Although this prosciutto is one of the common ingredients of Bolognese cooking, it is best eaten on its own with some unbuttered bread or grissini and a glass or two of slightly fizzy white wine.

A stall in Bologna, laden with aubergines of every shape and hue

VEAL ESCALOPES WITH
PARMA HAM AND CHEESE
Cotolette Alla Petroniana

6 veal escalopes
100g (4 oz) finaly grated Grana or Parmesan cheese
1 egg, beaten
salt
75g (3 oz) fresh breadcrumbs
60 ml (4 tbsp) olive oil
6 slices of prosciutto, cut into small pieces
6 slices of Emmental cheese
60ml (4 tbsp) beef stock
knob of butter
slivers of white truffle (optional)

SERVES 6

Lay the veal escalopes on a chopping board and beat lightly to tenderise them. Dust with a little of the grated cheese, then dip them in the beaten egg seasoned with salt, then a second time in the cheese, reserving the rest, and finally in the breadcrumbs.

Heat the oil in a wide frying pan, add the coated meat and fry until the outside is golden brown, turning once.

Remove the meat from the pan. Layer a slice of both prosciutto and Emmental cheese on to of each piece and dust with the remaining grated Grana or Parmesan cheese.

Lay them in a shallow flameproof casserole with the stock and butter, cover and cook for 2-3 minutes over a moderate heat. The cutlets should be tender but dry. Serve garnished with slivers of white truffle, if you have them.

BOLOGNESE SAUCE
Salsa Bolognese

30ml (2 tbsp) olive oil
1/2 onion, finely chopped
1 carrot, finely chopped
1 stick celery, finely chopped
450g (1 lb) beef, minced
200g (7 oz) veal, minced
100g (4 oz) pork, minced
300g (11 oz) canned plum tomatoes, sieved
5ml (1 tsp) tomato purée
750ml (1¼ pints) veal stock
300ml (½ pint) good red wine
1 bay leaf
salt

SERVES 10

Heat the oil in a large saucepan and sauté the onion, carrot and celery until softened.

Add the beef, veal and pork and sauté until browned. Remove any excess fat from the pan with a spoon.

Add the sieved tomatoes, stock, red wine and bay leaf. Leave to cook over a moderate heat for 1 hour, stirring frequently.

Season with salt before serving.

TORTELLINI IN BROTH
Tortellini in Brodo

It is recommended that the tortellini are prepared in the morning.

For the pasta
300g (11 oz) plain flour
3 eggs
salt

For the filling
50g (2 oz) butter
150g (5 oz) veal (possibly meat from around the noisette and contrefilet, cut into tiny dice)
100g (4 oz) pork loin, cut into small cubes
150g (5 oz) prosciutto
100g (4 oz) mortadella
2 large eggs, beaten
150-200g (5-7 oz) Grana cheese, grated
salt
grated nutmeg

For the broth
1kg (2¼ lb) shoulder of beef
1 free-range chicken
1 stick celery
1 carrot
1 onion
salt

SERVES 6

To make the pasta dough, put the flour in a large bowl, make a well in the centre and break in the eggs. Add a pinch of salt. Mix together into a dough and knead energetically for 15 minutes: it should be quite moist. Form the dough into a ball, wrap it in cling film and refrigerate for at least 30 minutes.

To make the filling, melt the butter in a frying pan and cook the cubes of veal and pork for 15-20 minutes until they are well browned. Remove the meat from the pan and leave it to cool. Then put it through mincer twice together with the cold meats. Put the minced meat into a bowl, add the beaten egg and the cheese, and season with salt and grated nutmeg. Mix all the ingredients together, cover with cling film and leave in the refrigerator for 12 hours.

To make the broth, put the meat and the chicken into a large saucepan and cover with cold water. Bring to the boil and then skim. Add the vegetables, season with salt and simmer slowly for at least 2 hours.

To make the tortellini, roll out the pasta dough very thinly and cut into squares about 3cm (1¹/₄ inches). Put a little of the filling in the centre of each square, then fold the pasta into a triangle, pressing down the edges to prevent the filling from escaping during cooking. Fold the tortellini around your index finger, overlapping the two corners, pressing well so that they stick together and keep their shape. Lay them out on a clean floured tea-towel.

Heat the freshly made broth (never use stock from the day before to cook the tortellini) in a large saucepan. When it is boiling, add the tortellini and simmer for about 3 minutes. Serve very hot.

Deft fingers make tortellini this small!

Around Emilia

Big and rich, Modena, the next city along the via Emilia from Bologna, is known to all automobile connoisseurs as the home of Maserati, De Tomaso and Ferrari, three of the most expensive and exotic motorcars made in Europe. The architectural grandeur of Modena reflects the wealth and power of the D'Este family who dominated Modena's politics for hundreds of years. Some British readers will be familiar with the city as the birthplace of Mary of Modena, wife of the unfortunate King James II. The bulk of Modena's most famous son, Luciano Pavarotti, hints that in Modena you can eat well. To gastronomes, gourmets and habitués of high priced delicatessens, Modena means one thing above all else: vinegar.

The characteristic vinegar of Modena is aceto balsamico, or balsamic vinegar, which has emerged as one of the trademarks of modern Italian cooking. The making of balsamic vinegar itself is ancient and mysterious. It begins with the juice of Trebbiano grapes, gently simmered. The sugary liquid is then aged in a series of barrels made from a variety of different woods – ash, cherry, chestnut and oak, for example. Every year some of the embryonic vinegar is moved from one barrel to another as complex enzyme reactions slowly turn the sugar in the grapes into acid.

Over decades the vinegar becomes more mellow and complex. Sometimes the process can go on for a hundred years. This is known as the artignale or artisani method of producing balsamic vinegar. The barrels are stored in the attics of the big farm houses and country estates of well-to-do Modena families. The vinegar is almost never sold: it forms a part of the dowry of many young Modenese women. Balsamico is also mass produced, and the industrial product can be either very good indeed or a shabby, one-dimensional travesty of its artisanal prototype.

Just to the south-east of Modena, the unremarkable town of Spilamberto is home of the Consorteria Dell' Aceto Balsamico Tradizionale, an organisation set up after the war to help families rebuild their stocks of balsamic that were destroyed by air raids or artillery fire, and also to safeguard the proper traditions of balsamic vinegar-making. I sat in on the Consorteria's deliberations when they held a formal tasting of balsamic vinegars. (Every year they award the best balsamic with a prize, the Palio di San Giovanni.) The vinegars are carefully, almost scientifically, judged on the basis of appearance, aroma and taste. Words and phrases like 'harmonious', 'pleasing', 'a bit cloudy', 'too dense' and 'rather modest' were quietly bandied around the tasting table, as the judges carefully filled in score sheets rating the vinegars. The best old balsamicos are thick, shiny and the colour of dark brown mink. They are vinegars that can be drunk – I should say sipped, as they are too precious to drink – like a cognac. They are used sparingly, just a few drops here and there, to give intense flavour to cooked vegetables, grills or even peaches. This sort of vinegar rarely gets sold, but if you could find some on the market, you would certainly pay well over £100 for a tiny bottle. If you are ever lucky enough to taste it you will know why 'balsamico' means 'a fragrant and healing ointment'.

You are more likely to get your hands on the industrially produced stuff which pours out of factories large and small all around Modena. Buy carefully and you will have a delightful and pungent addition to your salad dressings, a terrific flavouring for deglazing sauteed dishes and a first class condiment that's worth experimenting with. Just don't try to drink the stuff!

The other great product of Emilia is Parmesan cheese which somehow seems to find its way into every Italian dish. Indeed some cookery authorities have worried that the almost ubiquitous use of Parmesan has had a stultify-ing effect on Italian cooking. The cheese has had a high reputation for hundreds of years. One of my favourite authorities on Italian cookery, Anna del Conte, quotes the 14th century Decameron of Boccaccio: '...and on a mountain all of grated Parmesan cheese dwelt folk that did nought else, but make macaroni and ravioli'.

Parmesan is one of the most delicious and useful cheeses made anywhere in the world. Its official name is Parmigiano Reggiano. You may be able to buy Parmesan cheese made in Denmark, New Zealand or Wisconsin for all I know – the cheese is widely copied – but Parmigiano Reggiano is only made in Emilia-Romagna in the provinces of Modena, Parma, Bologna, Mantova and Reggio Emilia. There is a similar local cheese called Grana Padano which looks, grates and cooks like Parmesan, but it is not the same thing at all. There is only one Parmigiano Reggiano and you can easily recognise it in any shop because the name is stencilled in black all over the rind.

I must say at this stage that if you're not able to see the whole cheese or at least a substantial chunk of it, don't bother buying it. You can get small shrink-wrapped wedges of the real thing in most good supermarkets and they will be good, but they really won't approach the quality of a piece cut to your requirements as you watch. Little tubs of ready-grated parmesan are completely useless. It's time to reiterate that simple cooking requires the best ingredients. Don't cut corners on quality: in the long run the best is the cheapest and certainly the most delicious.

Parmigano Reggiano begins with cows: in the case of the dairy farm that I visited, a herd of lovely Pezzata Nera. The name literally means 'black stains' and refers to the cows' black and white colouring. The cows graze the lush slopes of the gently rolling countryside and their milk is sent to a number of small cheese-making factories. At the dairy, the milk is skimmed, fermented, moulded and salted. Parmigiano Reggiano requires a lot of milk – about 16 litres to make a kilogram of cheese. It requires a lot of time as well. A young Parmigiano Reggiano may be just under a year old, but a more mature cheese may be well over two years old. Because the cheeses have to age before they can be sold, the local dairy farmers and cheese-

Grated cheeses from the supermarket are no substitute for local produce

makers have an enormous amount of capital tied up in their aging cheeses. Banks in the area take the cheeses as collateral for loans; the cheeses are mortgaged as it were.

I visited one vast bank-owned warehouse, or maybe it ought to be called a cheese vault, where 110,000 cheeses, each weighing 30 kilograms, were quietly maturing at 17 degrees centigrade. A quick calculation told me that there total value was about £20 million.

If you've only ever used Parmesan for grating you're in for a revelation when you try it as table cheese. A little bit of Parmigiano Reggiano in good condition has the most delicate, nutty flavour and perfume, and it's absolutely fantastic with some ripe pears. It is also wonderful shaved thickly on to a salad of strong-tasting leaves like rocket, and dressed with a little truffle-infused olive oil or a balsamico and olive oil dressing.

At the cheesemaker I visited, one of the team took out his cotello mandello (the almond-shaped knife that cuts Parmesan most efficiently) and carved some chunks out of a middle-aged cheese that was just approaching its second birthday. The complex and seductive flavour is, like most of the flavours of Emilia-Romagna, incredibly powerful – it almost explodes in your mouth. If you find good Parmesan or if you're able to go to Italy, invest in a fairly substantial piece, big enough to last you for four to six weeks. It keeps well in the fridge, if it is wrapped in foil (which I prefer) or cling film.

The best food I ate in this region, of quite extraordinarily good food, was at the charming and eccentric little Villa Gaidello Club, a tiny restaurant with rooms converted from a group of farm buildings just outside Castelfranco Emilia about halfway between Bologna and Modena. The place is under the aegis of Paola Bini, an inspired cook and pioneering organic farmer. Almost everything you eat and drink here comes from Paola's fields, vegetable patches, orchards and vineyard.

Paola took us to look at the little bottling factory – or shed, really – where her team preserves tiny onions in balsamic vinegar. Big, spartan brick barns and farmhouses, which are really quite beautiful, dot the flat, fertile fields here. 'The architecture of the Emilian countryside is very different from what you find elsewhere in Italy,' Paola tells me, 'the architecture of Florence is elegant; the architecture of Bologna is grand; the architecture here is essential.'

The cooking in Paola's restaurant is 'essential' too. Back in the kitchen she showed me the simple characteristic flavours of Emilia: parsley, garlic and rosemary. 'Everything we cook and eat here is authentic and traditional,' she said. That evening in the conservatory-cum-dining room we sat down to find a stack of seven plates in front of each of us. As we learned during dinner, each course is served on the top plate of the stack which is removed as you finish the course. You go through the night with a decreasing stack of plates and an expanding waistline. There is a set menu and we were surprised and delighted with each course.

Dinner kicked off with onions in balsamic vinegar, a sweet and sour accompaniment to nutty prosciutto and little puffs of fried bread. Then a big bowl of delicate tortellini in a pale golden broth, followed by a plate of tagliatelle dressed with a fresh tomato and prosciutto sauce. Next course, an irreproachable roast rabbit of indescribable simplicity and deliciousness. Afterwards, little meatballs in a tangy balsamic sauce, and vegetables baked with breadcrumbs, Parmesan, parsley and garlic. Then the puddings arrived: fried egg custard paving the way for a rich and boozy trifle. The whole affair was washed down with lively local Lambrusco and we finished with little glasses of powerful walnut liqueur. 'Authentic and traditional' in Paula's words, and indeed one of the greatest meals ever.

Above: Good, simple cooking cannot be achieved without the finest ingredients. Peaches and grapes, grown to perfection, are displayed here

Right: Only a matter of hours separate these vegetables from picking to cooking

MEATBALLS WITH BALSAMIC VINEGAR
Polpettone all Aceto Balsamico

The meatballs can be served with a vegetable gratin.

100g (4 oz) soft breadcrumbs
milk
500g (18 oz) good quality minced beef
300g (11 oz) Grana cheese, grated
50g (2 oz) walnuts, chopped
2 eggs, beaten
salt and freshly ground black pepper
flour
corn oil for frying
butter
2 cloves garlic, crushed
30ml (2 tbsp) chopped parsley
60ml (4 tbsp) balsamic vinegar

SERVES 4

Put the breadcrumbs in a dish, cover with milk and leave to soak for 30 minutes. Then drain and mix with the beef, cheese, walnuts, eggs, salt and pepper. Form the mixture into small balls, roll in flour and fry in corn oil.

Melt a little butter in a roasting tin and fry the crushed garlic and parsley. Cook the meatballs gently in this mixture for a few minutes. Finally, add the balsamic vinegar and cook the meatballs for a few more minutes.

STUFFED BAKED VEGETABLES
Grattinata ai Legumi

Vegetables such as aubergines, courgettes, peppers and tomatoes, can be filled with this mixture, brushed with a little melted butter and baked at 180°C (350°F) mark 4 for 20 minutes.

100g (4 oz) fresh breadcrumbs
100g (4 oz) Grana cheese, grated
salt and freshly ground black pepper
1 clove garlic, crushed
15ml (1 tbsp) chopped fresh parsley

SERVES 4

Mix all the ingredients together thoroughly and use to stuff hollowed-out vegetables.

CARROT CAKE
Torta Carote

250g (9 oz) castor sugar
250g (9 oz) ground almonds
250g (9 oz) carrots, grated
15ml (1 tbsp) Amaretti
5 eggs, separated
1 sachet of easy-blend yeast
butter
plain white flour

Mix the sugar, almonds, carrots, Amaretti and egg yolks together. Whisk the egg whites until they form peaks and then fold them in lightly. Turn the mixture into a buttered and floured 25cm (10inch) round cake tin. Bake in the oven at 180°C (350°F) mark 4 for 45 minutes until a knife inserted into the centre comes out clean.

To Treviso

As you travel through Italy, foods come and go. You move from the region of olive oil into the region of butter, or from the region of dried pasta into the region of fresh pasta. Modern transport and communications mean that the old food regions are breaking down though: in Italy, as in Britain or the United States, an increasing number of people want to have everything available all the time and everywhere. This erosion of local, regional and seasonal culture is sad and ultimately impoverishing, but understandable. It is almost impossible to restrict the good things in life to a place, a season or just a few people.

Risotto is one of the good things in life and can be found – in more or usually less – authentic form in menus around the world and all over Italy. Whilst you can eat a perfectly good risotto in Positano, Castellina in Chianti, or in Rome, it is fundamentally a dish of the north. The risotto belt of Italy stretches from the Piedmont region in the west to the Veneto. If you have never eaten or cooked a real risotto, you are missing out on one of the great dishes of any cuisine.

You can't make a risotto without rice. Although rice was known in the ancient world, no one is really sure when it was brought to Italy or by whom: was it marauding Saracens, invading Spaniards or restless Venetians who established the grain here? Certainly it was being grown in Italy by Renaissance times, but risotto as a dish, didn't really begin its rise to popularity until the 19th century.

The River Po, the Amazon of Italy, begins in the high Alps near Turin and then meanders broad and powerful across Emilia before draining into the Adriatic sea. Rice grows particularly well in the broad marshy flatlands of the lower Po. The Italian rice production of one million tons a

Above: An unusual way to serve a pumpkin risotto!

Below: And for dessert, why not try a tempting grape tart

year seems trifling when you compare it to say, Thailand which produces 20 times as much of the stuff. But Italy is the biggest rice producer in Europe and also grows a huge range of rice from the useful, if unexciting, everyday rice, to the luxurious specialised round grains that feature in the best risotti.

My search for the superlative risotto rice took me to the rice-crazy town of Isola Della Scala, the self-described 'capital of vialone nano' (vialone nano may be to risotto rice what Lafite Rothschild is to red wine). The rice fields here are one of the few places in Italy where the vialone nano grows, and the lack of pesticides and herbicides in its production is testified by the gin-clear water, full of darting fish and furtive frogs, that flows through the fields.

The oldest rice mill hereabouts – and one of the oldest factories still operating in Italy – is the Antica Riseria Ferron which opened for business in 1656. In the mill, the old machines husk, pound, polish and sieve the rice. There are no chemicals and no high speed anything in the whole process. A scanty 90 kilograms of rice a day comes out of the mill, so vialone nano is a relatively high priced product. You may have seen many recipes advising arborio as the best risotto rice; well hereabouts vialone nano is king. Local cooks praise its flavour and versatility, and find it a slightly more 'forgiving' rice to cook with, than arborio.

Gabrielle Ferron, who runs the old family business, has demonstrated risotto cooking from Thailand to Chicago. He showed me the way risotto is made in Isola della Scala. Conventionally, you heat a little oil or butter in a saucepan, soften some chopped onion and then add your rice, frying it briefly until it becomes shiny. You then begin adding your stock very gradually, stirring all the time with a wooden spoon and slowly adding more liquid. After 20 or 25 minutes, the rice develops a creamy consistency. This is a dish that requires instinct and constant attention.

Here they do it differently, Gabrielle explained: they use two volumes of liquid for every volume of rice and leave the rice to cook, covered and unstirred. It is a method that certainly works, but only with vialone nano. Risotti here can be flavoured with the same frogs that live in the rice fields or cooked with pumpkin or something more exotic. Gabrielle produced an absolutely mind-boggling radicchio and prawn risotto that was gently spiked with curry powder. He also cooks a sensational risotto with green apples, and even makes a rice ice cream. Watching him move away from some of the many conventions of risotto cooking was inspirational and entertaining.

There was more rice on the menu when we took a major detour to visit the kitchens of the Villa del Quo and chatted with Gian Paolo Cagni, a chef who has devoted much of his career to preserving characteristic Mantuan cooking. The Mantuan region is squeezed between the Veneto and Emilia. Its cooking owes a lot to both regions, but nonetheless has its own distinctive and relatively unexported characteristics – it is a cuisine that hasn't really travelled. Cagni told us about some of the more unusual Mantuan specialities: bigoi con le sardelle (a hefty variety of spaghetti served with salted sardines), snail soup, frog surprise and, dare I mention it, stracotto d'asino (donkey stew). I looked forward to the spaghetti with sardines, but was a little daunted by the other dishes, so it was a relief when he presented a really magnificent looking and tasting torta di riso, a rice tart bursting with the festive tastes of candied fruit and rum.

We headed off into the Veneto, the province of Venice. Alas we passed by Verona, beloved for opera in the Roman amphitheatre, and a dozen sights that claim some connection with Romeo and Juliet (Shakespeare's lovers and their unreasonable relatives were all natives of Verona). If you're in this part of Italy be sure to stop there. But I was thrilled to be on my way to the less well visited Treviso.

Treviso is bustling, mercantile and fashionable. Benetton, Stefanel and some less celebrated Italian fashion and design houses have their headquarters in or near the city. The city's role as a fashion capital is an old one: weaving was well established in the Middle Ages and the area around Treviso became a centre for silk production in the 16th century. Modern day Treviso is celebrated for its

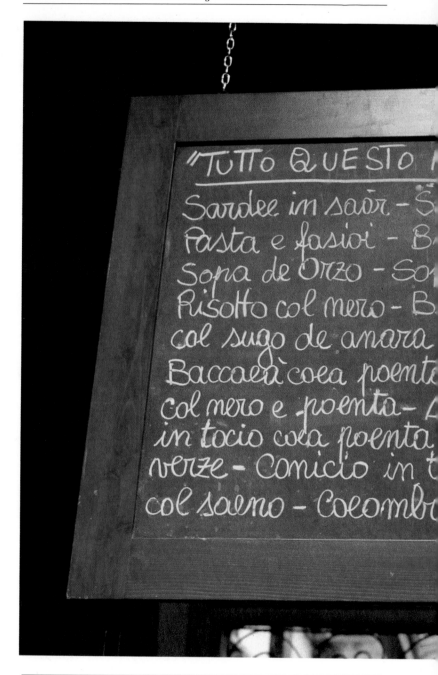

'All this not always' heads this menu of mouth-watering dishes in Treviso

cashmere scarves and lambswool sweaters, but it is also known as the 'citta dipinta' (the city of frescoes) and the 'citta d'acque' (the city of water).

The frescoes were once found all over central Treviso within the area of the city's 16th century walls: the painted plaster helped to protect the city's brick buildings from the ravages of the weather. Many of the frescoes are long gone, but look carefully and you will still be able to find cherubs, saints, old coat of arms and fanciful arabesques. The water refers to Treviso's extensive and picturesque system of canals which thread in and out of the local river, the Sile. If you like, you can travel along the Sile all the way to Venice.

Americans are likely to immediately recognise the culinary contribution of Treviso: in the United States, what we in Britain call radicchio, the strong tasting red chicory, is sometimes known as Treviso. There are two main types of radicchio – the round, slightly more common radicchio di Castelfranco and the long-leaved, rather sweeter radicchio di Treviso. Both leaves are at their best in the winter, although varieties of radicchio can now grow all year round and can be found in salads, risotti or as a filling for various pastas.

Radicchio is prized for its ravishing colour: it finds its way into a lot of non-Italian cooking on decorative merit alone. If you've been put off by the bitter taste, you probably haven't tasted the real radicchio de Treviso. But it's also worth knowing that as the radicchio cooks, the sweetness in its makeup becomes more pronounced. Radicchio risotto for example has an alluring but rather hard to define bitter-sweet quality.

Treviso's major culinary claim to fame at the moment, though, is as the birthplace of tiramisu, the Italian pudding whose meteoric ascent in popularity means that you can now buy little tubs of it in corner shops in London as well as in supermarkets throughout Britain. The name literally means 'pick me up' and probably refers to the use of cold, strong coffee in the recipe. Similar puddings which use mascarpone (a very white, rich and creamy cows' milk cheese) can be found throughout Italy. In these puddings the cheese may be combined with eggs, rum, sugar, candied fruit or biscuits. For some reason, tiramisu became the Italian pudding that conquered the world. Italians, by the way, do not eat puddings nearly as often as the British or Americans. A meal is usually finished off with some fruit: puddings tend to be for special occasions.

As far as I can tell, our modern tiramisu was 'invented' in the mid-sixties at the Beccherie, a most delightful old inn and restaurant a short stroll from Treviso's medieval town hall, the Palazzo dei Trecento. Many of the great dishes of the Veneto are on the menu here: I tasted some fascinating sardines 'in saor'. In saor is a very old method of cooking fish. The sardines are fried and then marinated in vinegar with onions, bay leaves and raisins. The result is a lovely and complex, sweet and sour flavour of the sort that you don't find in Italian cooking outside of Italy. I ate some delicious pumpkin gnocchi as well, but I was really there to meet Alba, whose mother Antonietta first made the pudding, tiramisu. She showed me how it's done. The ingredients are simple: espresso, savoyard (sponge finger) biscuits, cocoa, eggs and mascarpone. Unlike many variations of tiramisu which demand rum, Amaretto, Tia Maria or even brandy, Alba's recipe is booze-free.

'The one thing tiramisu must never have in it,' she proclaims, 'is alcohol.' I've eaten a lot of tiramisu – indeed enough to be rather bored with the stuff – but Alba's was really something else. The inherent richness of the dish was neatly balanced by flavours that were both clear and delicate. I ate a whole plateful.

TIRAMISU
Tiramisu

Neither the Savoy biscuits nor the mascarpone cream should be mixed with any kind of liqueur or spirit. The real Tiramisu has no spirits. Those made with spirits, in Italy and now elsewhere, are only unsuccessful imitations.

500ml (18 fl oz) hot, strong black coffee
6 egg yolks
150g (5 oz) caster sugar
300g (11 oz) mascarpone cheese
1 packet Savoy biscuits
cocoa powder

SERVES 6

Beat the egg yolks with the sugar. Add the mascarpone cheese, beating the mixture with a whisk.

Soak the Savoy biscuits briefly in the coffee.

Arrange a layer of the Savoy biscuits in a rectangular serving dish. Pour the mascarpone cheese mixture over the biscuits. Repeat with another layer of both Savoy biscuits and mascarpone cheese mixture. Dust the top with cocoa powder.

Alba's tiramisu was really something special

CREAMED SALT COD
Balcalà Mantecato

500g (18 oz) salt cod
1 litre (1³/₄ pints) water
1 litre (1³/₄ pints) milk
salt and freshly ground black pepper
250ml (8 fl oz) olive oil

SERVES 6

Soak the salt cod in the water overnight, then drain. Mince the salt cod. Put the minced fish in a large saucepan and boil with the milk for 1 hour. Do not add any salt. Place in a strainer to drain off the liquid. Put the fish in a saucepan and work it preferably with a balloon whisk, adding the olive oil very slowly. Continue until you obtain a homogeneous mixture. Season with salt and pepper.

RADICCHIO SOUP
Zuppa di Radicchio di Treviso

125ml (4 fl oz) extra virgin olive oil
1 medium-sized onion, finely chopped
1kg (1¹/₄ lb) radicchio
salt and freshly ground black pepper

SERVES 4

Heat the olive oil in a large saucepan and cook the onion, being careful only to let it sweat – do not brown it.

Separate the leaves of the radicchio, then wash and dry them. Cut out the core and chop the leaves.

Put the chopped radicchio into the saucepan, season with salt and pepper, cover with cold water and bring to the boil then cook slowly for 2 hours and serve piping hot.

RICE ICE CREAM
Gelato di Riso

250g (9 oz) ground rice or rice flour
pinch of salt
grated rind of 2 lemons
1 litre (1³/₄ pints) milk
8 eggs, separated
300g (11 oz) caster sugar
500g (18 oz) mascarpone cheese
about 5ml (1 tsp) vanilla essence
250g (9 oz) Amaretti macaroons, crushed

SERVES 20

Put the semolina of rice or rice flour in a saucepan with the salt, lemon rind and milk.

Cook over a low heat for about 25 minutes, stirring occasionally, until the mixture is thick and smooth. Leave until cold.

Beat the egg yolks with the sugar until pale and creamy. Add the mascarpone cheese and mix thoroughly.

Whisk the egg whites until peaks form and add the vanilla essence. Fold the mascarpone cheese mixture into the egg whites gently but thoroughly. Add the rice mixture with the crushed macaroons.

Spoon the rice mixture into a shallow freezer container. Freeze for about 2 hours and serve chilled.

Traditional pots and pans on display

RICE WITH GORGONZOLA CHEESE AND SPINACH
Risotto con Gorgonzola e Spinaci

30ml (2 tbsp) extra virgin olive oil

a few slices of onion, finely chopped

1 clove garlic, finely chopped

400g (14 oz) spinach, cooked and chopped

salt and freshly ground black pepper

400g (14 oz) risotto rice

800ml (28 fl oz) vegetable stock

250g (9 oz) Gorgonzola cheese, crumbled

Heat the olive oil in a large frying pan and sauté the onion and garlic for 2-3 minutes. Add the spinach and season with salt and pepper. Stir in the rice and cook it for 2-3 minutes over a moderately high heat. Add the stock, stir gently and lower the heat. Leave to cook for about 15 minutes, or until tender. Then stir in the Gorgonzola cheese gently and let it melt before serving.

In and out of the Alps

L eaving Treviso we turned away from Venice – an easy hour's drive – and headed across the broad, flatlands of the Veneto towards the Dolomites, the Italian region of the South Tirolese Alps. Although these mountains were first popularised by 19th century English hikers and mountaineers, today they are a favourite destination for German and Austrian tourists. We pulled off the motorway at the busy town of Trento, or Trent.

Catholics, and the historically-minded, will be familiar with Trent as the setting for the mid-16th century Council of Trent, where the Catholic church marshalled its theological forces against the then new and aggressively expansionist Protestant churches. The traditional Latin mass, the Tridentine Mass, takes its name from Tridentum, the Roman name for Trent. We shall return to religion later.

As night fell we sped, then crawled, along the steepest, most twisted and menacing of all of Italy's steep, twisted and menacing mountain roads. The short – by the map – distance we had to travel stretched out into a long and tiring journey as we threaded through the dense, black mountain landscape. Very late in the evening we arrived at the ski resort of Pinzolo from where we were guided to our chalet about a further 45 minutes away, mostly uphill. We arrived very late and very hungry at a beautiful house called Maso Doss where we were greeted by a blazing fire and the smell of good cooking.

The Trentino region of Italy is really quite extraordinary. It is Alpine; it was Austrian until 1918, and its physical appearance, culture and some of its food make you think that you're not in Italy. Its sister region, the Alto Adige, is even more Germanic. There, the names of towns are proclaimed on roadsides and railway stations in both

Italian and German, and German is the language of daily life. The cooking of the Alto Adige is German as well. Here in the Trentino the cooking has hints of both Venice and Vienna. At Maso Doss we were warmly greeted by our host and hostess and settled around a big pine table. A sign on the wall read: 'A Filippo chef provetto tutto il nostra grande affetto'. It was a testimony from some previous guests praising the culinary skills of Filippo who, I was pleased to see, was in the kitchen putting the finishing touches to our late dinner. As we moved from dish to dish it was clear that this was a land of the dairy, pigs and polenta.

Polenta is made from finely ground maize. If you have never eaten it or seen it, I suppose that it can best be described as a sort of porridge. It is after all made in much the same way. It is rather more versatile though. You can eat it when it's hot and soft, or wait till it cools and cut it into thin slices which can be fried or grilled. In the mountains where food was scanty and life was hard, cheap and versatile polenta became the staple of existence.

Sitting around the table on our first night we ate little cubes of local cows' milk cheese, polenta with sauerkraut, peverada (a type of bread sauce heavily spiked with black pepper) and a very arcane local speciality, pagnoc. Pagnoc is a rather rich and fatty fried potato cake which I imagine is just the ticket if you've spent all day on a freezing mountainside rounding up the cows: it gives you an immediate shot of warmth and energy. It is not perhaps the ideal food for slimmers, the finicky or the overly delicate. All the food we ate that night was hearty and dished up in gargantuan helpings. Then the drinking began.

This is a great area for grappa, the fiery and exceptionally powerful spirit distilled from the remnants of grapes that have been crushed for wine-making. The stuff comes in a huge range of flavours, and the favourites at Maso Doss were honey and nettle. The grappa was beautifully made with a really rather delicate bouquet and pale gold colour that completely belied its lethal 40 per cent alcohol content. A sip or two was more than enough – even writing

The delicious flavour of these wild porcini is a far cry from that of the cultivated mushroom

about it gives me a headache. But I could understand how it might be just the short, sharp shock your digestive system craves after a big, rich, starchy meal.

The next morning we awoke in the midst of utterly ravishing and majestic mountain scenery and began to explore the local towns and valleys. The Val Rendena is the relatively wide valley where Pinzolo and the more important resort of Madonna di Campiglio are located. The valley is sprinkled with tiny villages and a surprising number of enormous churches, which brings us back to religion and history.

The city of Trent sits on the important ancient trade route linking the major centres of Verona in the south and Innsbruck to the north, over the Brenner pass. Because of Trent's wealth and relative isolation, the Bishops of Trent began to acquire considerable power and privileges –

rather like the Bishops of Durham in England – and ruled Trent as princes as well as spiritual leaders. They also oversaw the building of grandiose churches throughout their diocese, glorifying God and themselves in even the smallest villages. Many of the churches around here have striking and slightly spooky murals painted on their outside walls. Not far from Maso Doss, the church of San Vigilio is decorated with a really breathtaking 16th century fresco depicting the Dance of Death.

We also trekked into the absolutely ravishing Val Genova, which is a paradise for connoisseurs of waterfalls, cold and almost unbelievably blue mountain streams and picture postcard Alpine scenery. This majestic and quite remarkably unspoilt landscape is heavily protected by national parks. Unsurprisingly, the purity of the local water has been turned into a big business: Surgiva water, which springs

An excellent fish terrine served at Lake Lugano

from an 1,100 metre high glacial source, is bottled in a shiny new factory in the valley and shipped to an increasing number of fashionable restaurants around the world. The other Trentino product which finds its way around the world is wine. We weren't really on a wine trek so we gave the vineyards a miss, but Trentino wines – which tend to be 'varietal' which means based on a single grape rather than a blend – have become some of Italy's trendiest exports. The worldwide demand for wines made from Chardonnay, which grows particularly well here, has given Trentino wine-makers a huge boost. At least half the white grapes grown here are Chardonnay, although the grape was only introduced to the Trentino at the turn of the century. I must confess that I'm a little bored by Chardonnay these days, but I am completely in love with the terrific dry white wines that are made from Riesling or Pinot Grigio grapes in the Trentino.

Back at the house, Ugo Caola gave me a demonstration of traditional polenta-making. The 'rules' dictate that polenta ought to be made in a copper pot hanging over a wood fire. The pot was filled with water and when the water boiled he added the polenta in a thin, golden stream. Then the hard work began, because the polenta cook needs dedication and vigilance: the stuff has to be stirred constantly as it cooks, which takes about half an hour, to produce a silky smooth and even-textured polenta.

The stirring is done with a special stick known in local dialect as a 'trisa'. The trisa is carved from any number of soft woods, but reputedly the best trisa is one made from juniper which is said to infuse the polenta with a particularly delicate flavour. Polenta-making and eating is so important in this part of Italy that this valley, the Val Rendena, is familiarly known as the Val dala Trisa, or the valley of polenta-stirring sticks.

When the polenta was ready, Ugo poured it out on to a flat, wooden board called a 'tavel' where it cooled and thickened. For supper that night we ate massive slabs of polenta topped with delicious sauteed wild mushrooms from the nearby woods. Grappa inevitably followed.

The next morning we headed south as the sun rose over the glaciers and the Alpine landscape quickly dropped away as we hit the northern shores of Lake Garda, the largest of all the Italian lakes. In contrast to the harsh ferocity of the weather in the mountains, the Garda climate is gentle, clement and warm enough for lemons to grow. From Roman times, Garda has been a celebrated source of fish and on my brief jaunt with one of the local fishermen we caught a really handsome pike and a number of less well-known fish. We took these to the excellent Vecchia Lugana restaurant on the southern shore of the 30-mile-long lake where they were made into the best-looking fish pâté I've seen in a long time. It was also one of the most delicious: unlike a lot of fish pâtés which taste like nothing more than grown-up baby food, this one was a confident and really quite complex medley of flavours and textures, a real triumph.

GARDESAN FISH TERRINE WITH SPRING VEGETABLE AND HERB SAUCE
Terrina de Pesce Gardesano alle Verdure Primaverili con Salsa di Erbe Fini

300g (12 oz) red mullet fillets
60ml (4 tbsp) fish stock
150g (5 oz) trout fillets
150g (5 oz) salmon fillet
150g (5 oz) sardines, filleted
50g (2 oz) carrots
50g (2 oz) courgettes
50g (2 oz) spinach
50g (2 oz) potatoes
salt and freshly ground black pepper

For the sauce
90ml (6 tbsp) of mayonnaise
15ml (1 tbsp) cognac
30ml (2 tbsp) double cream
1 sprig rosemary, finely chopped
1 sage leaf, finely chopped
a bunch of chives, finely chopped
30ml (2 tbsp) parsley, finely chopped
30ml (tbsp) fennel, finely chopped

SERVES 6

Cut the vegetables into strips and blanch them in salted water. Drain and leave to cool.

Line a 900g (2 lb) terrine mould with foil and layer with the red mullet letting it go up the sides. Moisten with a teaspoon of the stock. Continue alternating layers of each fish and the vegetables, finishing with a layer of red mullet. Cover the mould with foil and stand it in a roasting tin half-filled with water. Bake in the oven at 180°C (350°F) mark 4 for about 1 hour. Remove from the oven and drain the cooking juices by pressing another mould on the top.

Leave to cool and then refrigerate for 24 hours.

Meanwhile, prepare the sauce by mixing all the ingredients together.

Cut the terrine into slices and arrange on dinner plates. Garnish with mixed lettuce leaves and the sauce. Serve with toast.

Fresh fish on sale in a local market

PIKE WITH BABY SPINACH AND BLACK OLIVES
Luccio con Spinaci Novelle e Citronette alle Olive Nere

4 pike steaks, about 175g (6 oz) each
600ml (1 pint) fish stock
200g (7 oz) baby spinach leaves, blanched

For the citronette
handful of fresh parsley
handful of fresh basil
60ml (4 tbsp) extra virgin olive oil
1 ripe tomato, peeled and finely chopped
juice of 1 lemon
5ml (1 tsp) coriander seeds, lightly crushed
6 black olives, chopped
salt and freshly ground black pepper

SERVES 4

Place the pike steaks in a steamer, cook them over fish stock until tender. Keep them hot.

Wash and dry the parsley and basil, then chop finely and put into a bowl. Add the olive oil, tomato, lemon juice, coriander seeds and black olives. Season with salt and pepper. Arrange some spinach leaves on each plate, lay the pike steaks on top and pour over the citronette.

CHEESE AND BACON SOUP
Pagnoc

25g (1 oz) lard
50g (2 oz) bacon, diced
50g (2 oz) salami, diced
100g (4 oz) 'spresse' cheese
6 potatoes, boiled and drained, then diced

Melt the lard in a frying pan and fry the bacon and salami until crisp. Add the cheese and the potatoes. Cook all the ingredients together over a moderate heat for 15-20 minutes.

FISH STOCK
Fume di Pesce

25g (1 oz) butter
50g (2 oz) onion, chopped
500-750g (1½-2 lb) fish bones, cleaned
2 sprigs thyme
1 bay leaf
¼ small stick celery
20g (³/₄ oz) sprigs parsley
5ml (1 tsp) white peppercorns
1 litre (1³/₄ pints) water
fine salt

Melt the butter in a large saucepan, add the onion and let it sweat for 5 minutes. Add the fish bones with the thyme, bay leaf, celery and parsley bound together securely with thread, and the peppercorns. Cook for about 5 minutes, stirring constantly. Add the water, bring to the boil and skim, then simmer over a low heat for 20 minutes. Strain the stock through a conical sauce sieve.

DUMPLING SOUP
Canederli in Brodo

4 bread rolls
1 egg
20ml (4 tsp) hot milk
100g (4 oz) plain flour
10ml (2 tsp) chopped parsley
1 fresh, large lugince or other fresh sausage, chopped
600ml (1 pint) beef stock

SERVES 4

Break up the bread rolls into little pieces. Soak them in hot milk for 10 minutes. Mix with egg, flour and parsley.

Form the mixture into little balls. Bring stock to the boil in a large pan, add dumplings and simmer for 15 minutes.

Through the doors of the famous Harry's Bar, you can sample sublime Carpaccio

To Venice

Whether you visit Venice for the first or the fiftieth time, it surprises, delights and amazes every time. In spite of pollution, neglect and decay, Venice remains – for me at any rate – the most beautiful city in the world. It has a rather bad reputation for food. A lot of this is because the pressures and profits of mass tourism tend to corrupt. If you are a restaurateur with a clientele who are entirely transient, have plenty of money and are unlikely ever to come back again, you really don't have to put too much effort into cooking or hospitality. It is, alas, the same in any of the great tourist destinations. It is too easy to eat, and indeed sleep, badly in Venice, but it is a city with some of the best hotels in the world and some of my favourite restaurants. I also feel that a lot of Italians find Venetian food tiresome, although some of that feeling might be due to envy of centuries of Venetian airs and graces.

Food formed the basis of the city's wealth. The very first settlers came to this scattering of tiny islands in the lagoon looking for a safe heaven from the dangers, chaos and terror of the last days of the Roman empire. Isolated but industrious, they began to produce salt. As an early historian pointed out: 'Not everyone wants to look for gold; on the other hand none can do without salt: all food needs this condiment to be agreeable to our taste... For this reason the great occupation of the Venetians is working in the salt pans... and from this work of salt production they can buy everything else that they need which they cannot produce.'

Spices were important too, as Venice grew and prospered from its position as the gateway to Byzantium, the Arab world and Asia beyond. Any number of new tastes were first introduced to Europe by the merchants of Venice and a number of contemporary Venetian dishes continue to reflect the city's historic links with the East. For example, the sour-sweet flavours of sardines in saor – which we tasted in closeby Treviso – are clearly influenced by Middle Eastern taste. As you sit in St. Mark's Square – described by someone as the grandest drawing room in Europe – and sip an espresso at Florians, the most glamourous, snobbiest and expensive coffee bar to be found anywhere, you can consider the fact that the European tradition of pausing for a little cup of coffee began right here.

It is impossible to talk about Venice and not mention money, especially if you have just paid an astonishingly hefty bill for your espresso and an amusing biscuit or two. Venice can be a dizzyingly expensive city: it is after all a question of supply and demand. If everyone in the world wants to visit Venice – and if you're ever in the city in June or July, you will think that everyone in the world has arrived – they should of course pay heavily for the privilege and thereby enrich the shopkeepers, restaurant owners, souvenir sellers and concierges of the city.

But there are some bargains lurking. Venetians themselves have to eat, and are not always able or inclined to pay the bills for lunch or dinner at one of the city's more eminent establishments every day. So they tend to patronise rather less formal places called 'osterias'. A Venetian friend led us through a labyrinth of back streets away from the crowds of St. Mark's to what he said was a typical Venetian osteria called Al Mascaron. It was an unprepossessing little bar with a few tables, and as soon as I crossed the threshold I knew that the food was going to be really good.

The menu was a hand-written litany of emblematic Venetian dishes – polenta with squid, liver and onions, sardines in saor and so on. The cooking by Giancarlo Seno was fabulous and the prices by Venetian standards were bargain basement. Some of our fellow diners were having a full blown lunch, while others were indulging in that favourite Venetian pastime of a glass of wine and some cichetti, the Venetian dialect word for snacks.

Even this little restaurant had seven different fresh fish

on the menu and if you're a fish eater – as I am – Venice is one of the great gastronomic destinations. Wandering around the handsome and fascinating fish market just off the Grand Canal one morning, I was completely dazzled by the varieties and quality of fish and seafood on offer. I really hadn't seen anything like it since Bangkok. There were the tiniest, most delicate looking squid you can imagine as well as the most galumphing turbots; there was also an encyclopaedic array of scampi, prawns, shrimps and other seductive crustaceans including the entrancing little crayfish-like canoce.

If you want to sample a vast array of these creatures, you must go and have the buffet lunch at the Cipriani Hotel, a place of immense comfort, privacy and professionalism, although hardly for the faint-walleted. The kitchen there also produced the most devastatingly good pumpkin risotto in town. At the Cipriani you will drink the characteristic cocktails of Venice, such as Bellinis (champagne and crushed peaches) or Tizianos (champagne and crushed grapes), two of the many inspired gastronomic innovations of the Cipriani family now headed by Arrigo 'Harry' Cipriani.

The family used to own the Cipriani Hotel but they sold out years ago, and Harry is now based at the most famous bar in the world, Harry's Bar. You should know that the bar was not named after Harry: it was founded by his father and called Harry's in tribute to an American friend who lent him the money to set up the business. Now having dispensed with onomastic matters we might talk about the place itself. With complete unoriginality I can say that it is one of the tiny handful of places that I would unhesitatingly name as one of the best restaurants in the world.

It is completely without pretension, razzmatazz or frills. The ground floor bar is vaguely reminiscent of a not-too-grand thirties ocean liner. The upstairs dining room is comfortable and there's not much more to say about it, except that if you look up from your plate and out the window you will be mesmerised by the most beautiful of all

Al Mascaron, a typical Venetian osteria, where the locals can enjoy wonderful food

views: across the expanse of the Canale di San Marco to the island church of San Giorgio Maggiore. This is the most heavenly of all the heavenly churches designed by Andrea Palladio, the great 16th century architect who lived and worked mostly in nearby Vicenza on the mainland.

One of the loveliest things about Harry's is the menu, which gives you the day's weather forecast and a tantalising mix of bar food including a very superior club sandwich, Venetian classics and Harry's Bar specialties. Probably the most popular dish invented here, and now an essential item on the menus of the world's trendiest restaurants, is the simple and sublime Carpaccio. Like the famous cocktails, it is named after a Venetian painter, Vittore Carpaccio. The dish was first served in 1950 to mark the big Carpaccio exhibition in the city.

Simply delicious - Venetian-style liver served with soft, warm polenta

After lunch at Harry's you can have a short 'digestif' walk to the Accademia, Venice's major art gallery, and admire Vittore Carpaccio's *Legend of Saint Ursula,* or you can be slightly more adventurous and take a longer walk to the less crowded Scuola di San Giorgio degli Schiavoni and enjoy half an hour or so of delightful contemplation, in the company of some of Carpaccio's most entrancing paintings.

Back to Carpaccio the dish, which is 'merely' chilled, thinly sliced raw beef drizzled with a mixture of mayonnaise, Worcester sauce, lemon juice and a little milk. Its simplicity is its genius. If you go to Harry's Bar you must order it. But you must also order one of Harry's risotti and Harry's chicken salad and the brilliantly subtle fried scampi and... and... and... You might have to make more than one visit.

It is appropriate that so many of Harry's famous dishes pay tribute to artists because, in Venice in particular, and in Italy in general, art and food are often subtly intermingled. The English architect Caroline Mauduit writes about Palladio that he was always 'finding new ways of producing that cool, harmonious balance in a building which we all intuitively recognise to be right'. You can say the same about Italy's best cooks who produce a cuisine of simplicity, harmony and balance that invites you to enjoy; a cuisine that is just as vital to a harmonious and balanced life as any other art.

CIPRIANI CHICKEN SALAD
Insalata Di Pollo Cipriani

500g (18 oz) boiled chicken, cut into julienne
100g (4 oz) white celery, cut into julienne
a few drops of Worcestershire sauce
juice of 1 lemon
about 150ml (¼ pint) mayonnaise
salt and freshly ground black pepper
4 green lettuce leaves
2 tomatoes, sliced
1 hard-boiled egg, sliced
4 small crisp lettuce leaves
4 black olives

SERVES 4

Put the chicken and celery in a stainless steel bowl. Add the Worcestershire sauce, lemon juice and as much mayonnaise as is needed to coat lightly. Season with salt and pepper and mix the ingredients together carefully.

Cut the green lettuce leaves into julienne and arrange them in nests on four plates.

Divide the chicken salad between the nests. Garnish each one with slices of tomato and hard-boiled egg, then add a crisp lettuce leaf and place a black olive on top of the salad.

VEAL CASSEROLE WITH VEGETABLES
Stinco di Vitello al Legumi

100ml (3½ fl oz) olive oil
1 leg of veal
1 onion, finely chopped
2 cloves garlic, chopped
100ml (3½ fl oz) dry Marsala
100ml (3½ fl oz) dry white wine
500g (18 oz) carrots, chopped
500g (18 oz) green celery, chopped
500g (18 oz) new potatoes, chopped
500g (18 oz) baby courgettes, chopped
1 bay leaf
1 sprig fresh rosemary
1 sprig fresh sage
10ml (2 tsp) chopped fresh oregano
salt and freshly ground black pepper

SERVES 4

Heat the oil in a large flameproof casserole and cook the veal and onion until nearly golden brown. Add the garlic, cook for 2-3 minutes and pour over the Marsala.

Place in the oven at 190°C (375°F) mark 5 and cook for about 1½ hours, stirring occasionally and sprinkling with the wine.

Remove from the oven and add the vegetables and herbs. Season with salt and pepper and cook for a further 30 minutes.

Serve hot.

A creamy pumpkin risotto

RISOTTO WITH PUMPKIN
Risotto Di Zucca

200g (7 oz) butter
500g (18 oz) pumpkin, cut into small cubes
1 clove garlic
1 sprig rosemary
salt and freshly ground black pepper
¹/₂ onion, chopped
275g (10 oz) risotto rice
about 900ml (1¹/₂ pints) chicken stock
150g (5 oz) Parmesan cheese, grated

SERVES 4

Melt 100g (4 oz) of the butter in a large saucepan. Add the pumpkin, garlic and rosemary. Season with salt and pepper. Cook over a moderate heat until the pumpkin is tender.

Melt 50g (2 oz) of the remaining butter in another pan and fry the onion until it is lightly browned. Add the rice and cook until lightly browned, then add about 60ml (4 tbsp) stock and bring to the boil. Add more stock from time to time. When the rice is half-cooked, add the pumpkin mixture.

When the rice is cooked, remove from the heat and stir in the remaining butter and Parmesan cheese. If necessary season with more salt and pepper before serving.

SLICED BEEF WITH MAYONNAISE SAUCE
Carpaccio Cipriani

This is not a classic dish but was created in the early 1960s by Commendatore Giuseppe Cipriani, to mark the launching of the great Carpaccio exhibition in Venice. It was served as the first course at an official banquet held at the Hotel Cipriani.

The beef used for this recipe should be raw, very red and tender and should be cut from the sirloin rather than from the fillet. Cooling the meat facilitates its slicing but it must never be sliced when frozen as this can result in pools of water appearing on the plates. The sauce is served separately.

300g (11 oz) very lean roast beef, cut into thin slices
300ml (^{1}/$_2$ pint) mayonnaise
15ml (1 tbsp) Worcestershire sauce
2.5ml (^{1}/$_2$ tsp) dry mustard
juice of ^{1}/$_4$ lemon
a few drops of Tabasco
salt and freshly ground black pepper
75ml (3 fl oz) consommé

SERVES 4

Arrange the slices of meat so that they cover each plate.

To make the sauce, blend the remaining ingredients together, stirring thoroughly.

VENETIAN-STYLE LIVER
Fegato alla Veneziana

500g (1¼) calves' liver
30ml (2 tbsp) water
30ml (2 tbsp) wine vinegar
50ml (2 fl oz) vegetable oil
25g (1 oz) butter
500g (1¼ lb) onions, sliced
salt and freshly ground black pepper
a little lemon juice
30ml (2 tbsp) chopped fresh parsley

SERVES 4

Slice the calves' liver into thin strips and marinate in a mixture of water and vinegar for at least 1 hour.

Heat the oil and butter in a frying pan, then the onion on a low heat for 40-50 minutes until translucent and soft, stirring frequently. Add the strips of liver and cook them quickly. Season with salt and pepper and when the liver is almost cooked, add lemon juice and sprinkle with chopped parsley. Serve hot with soft, warm polenta.

GREEN APPLE AND POTATO PUREE
Purée di Patate alla Mela Verde

500g (18 oz) potatoes
25g (1 oz) butter
salt
60-90ml (4-6 tbsp) hot milk
1 Granny Smith apple

SERVES 4

Cook the potatoes in boiling water until tender. Drain, then pass through a sieve, add the butter and season with salt. Mix together thoroughly, adding enough hot milk to make a soft purée. Peel the apple and cut into cubes; add to the potato purée just before serving.

VEAL NOISETTES WITH CEPS
Nocette di Vitello al Funghi Porcini

30ml (2 tbsp) olive oil
250g (9 oz) fresh ceps
2 cloves garlic
45ml (3 tbsp) chopped fresh parsley
50g (2 oz) butter
a little plain flour for dusting
8 veal noisettes, about 60g (2½ oz) each
salt and freshly ground black pepper
60ml (4 tbsp) dry white wine

SERVES 4

Heat the oil in a large frying pan and cook the ceps with garlic and parsley until tender, then set aside.

Using a copper frying pan, heat 30ml (2 tbsp) of the oil with 25g (1 oz) of the butter. When it becomes slightly golden, add the lightly floured noisettes and cook for 2-3 minutes. Turn the meat over, season with salt and pepper and cook the other side in the same way. Remove the noisettes from the pan and keep warm.

Skim off the fat from the cooking jucies, pour over the dry white wine and let it reduce slightly. Add the ceps mixture and cook for a few more minutes.

Arrange the veal noisettes on a serving dish. Add the remaining butter to the sauce, then spoon it over the noisettes. Serve garnished with potato and green apple purée.